The Private Inve

MW01256967

By _____ Kissian

Copyright © 2023 Brandy Lane Publishing, LLC

Chapter 1: Introduction

Chapter 2: Why Become a Private Investigator?

Occupational Outlook for Private Investigators

Job Prospects

Salary Range

Typical Work Environment

Chapter 3: Education Requirements

Degree Programs

Continuing Education

Examination Requirements

Chapter 4: Training Requirements

Prior Experience

Private Investigator Training Programs

    Blue Ribbon Investigative Institute

    Private Investigator Training and Security Training Program

Firearms Training

On the Job Training

Chapter 5: Overview of State Licensing Requirements

Additional Requirements

Typical Reasons for Application Denial

Reciprocity Agreements

Other Uses for State Licensing Websites

Chapter 6: Licensing Requirements by State

Alabama

Alaska

Arkansas

California

Colorado

Connecticut

Delaware

Hawaii

Idaho

Illinois

Indiana

Iowa

Kansas

Louisiana

Maine

Maryland

Massachusetts

Michigan

Minnesota

Mississippi

Missouri

Montana

Nebraska

Nevada

New Hampshire

New Jersey

New Mexico

New York

North Carolina

North Dakota

Ohio

Oklahoma

Oregon

Pennsylvania

Rhode Island

South Carolina

South Dakota

Tennessee

Texas

Utah

Vermont

Virginia

Washington

Washington D.C.

West Virginia

Wisconsin

Wyoming

Chapter 7: Getting Your Business Up and Running

Chapter 8: State Private Investigator Associations

List of State Private Investigator Associations

Alabama

Alaska

Arizona

Arkansas

California

Colorado

Connecticut

Delaware

Florida

Georgia

Idaho

Illinois

Indiana

Iowa

Kansas

Kentucky

Louisiana

Maine

Maryland

Massachusetts

Michigan

Minnesota

Mississippi

Missouri

Montana

Nebraska

New Hampshire

New Jersey

New York

North Dakota

Ohio

Oklahoma

Oregon

Rhode Island

South Carolina

Tennessee

Texas

Utah

Vermont

Virginia

Other Industry Associations

Chapter 9: Conclusion

About the Author

Disclaimers

Limit of Liability and Disclaimer of Warranty

Trademarks

Chapter 1: Introduction

Think you might be interested in pursuing a career as a private investigator? Browse the pages of this book to learn how and where to get the necessary training and education from start to finish. You'll learn about the licensing requirements and application process for all 50 states. You'll also learn where to get help setting your business in motion, including assistance with essential marketing, website setup, and professional association networking.

If you're already a private investigator, this book can help you to expand your services into other states. You can use it as a quick reference for getting licensed, developing your credentials, and establishing a referral network. Likewise, agencies can provide a copy to new employees to help guide them through the licensing and application process.

In short, if you're ready to embark on your path to becoming a private investigator, then you've found the right place to start.

Chapter 2: Why Become a Private Investigator?

A licensed private investigator uncovers facts and information, finds missing persons, and gathers evidence for private citizens, corporations, and other agencies. Private investigators also work for attorneys and lawyers to resolve civil and criminal court cases. Still, other investigators work for insurance companies to review suspicious or fraudulent insurance claims. And many investigators play a crucial role for spouses seeking confirmation of adultery or other illegal conduct to establish grounds for a divorce.

Other types of private investigator activities include:

• Subcontracting with government agencies to uncover crimes or threats against the United States

• Determining the identity, habits, conduct, movements, whereabouts, affiliations, associations, transactions, reputation, or character of any society, person, or group of persons

• Ascertaining the credibility of witnesses or other persons, such as potential employees
Locating missing persons, owners of abandoned or escheated property, or heirs to estates
• Locating or recovering lost or stolen property
• Determining causes of fires, libels, slanders, losses, accidents, damages, or injuries to real or personal property

• Securing evidence to be used by investigating committees, boards of award, arbitration, or trial of civil and criminal cases

View a more comprehensive list of the types of services and activities a private investigator performs at https://www.einvestigator.com/private-investigator-services/.

Most states require private investigators to be licensed; some may be permitted to carry a firearm. Some detectives have prior military experience, and many worked as police officers or law enforcement officials. PIs keep detailed notes and records during each case and often testify in court regarding their observations on behalf of their clients.

Private investigators often work irregular hours, especially when conducting surveillance (e.g., sitting outside a subject's house during early morning hours hoping to get a photograph or video of their activity).

Many investigators provide process serving services, which is the delivery of subpoenas and other legal documents to parties involved in a legal case. Many detective agencies specialize in a particular field of expertise. For example, some agencies deal only in skip tracing related to finding missing persons or tracking down debtors. Others may specialize in technical surveillance countermeasures involving locating and dealing with electronic surveillance (for example, an electronically bugged boardroom for industrial espionage purposes).

Increasingly, investigators prefer to be known as "professional investigators." This may be a response to the sometimes negative image attributed to the P.I. profession and an effort to establish the industry as a proper and respectable profession.

For more information on the private investigation profession, please refer to the Bureau of Labor Statistics, U.S. Department of Labor, Occupational Outlook Handbook, Private Detectives and Investigators on the Internet at http://www.bls.gov/ooh/protective-service/private-detectives-and-investigators.htm.

Occupational Outlook for Private Investigators

According to the U.S. Department of Labor Occupational Outlook Handbook, the employment of private detectives and investigators is projected to grow 8 percent from 2019 to 2029, much faster than the average for all occupations. Demand for private detectives and investigators will stem from security concerns and the need to protect confidential information. Intense competition can be expected for jobs.

Technological advances have increased cybercrimes, such as identity theft, credit card fraud, and email spamming. Internet scams and other financial and insurance fraud create demand for investigative services, particularly in the legal services industry.

Background checks will continue to be a source of work for many investigators because employers and personal contacts wish to verify a person's credibility. The increasing popularity of online dating has led to an increase in men and women wanting to learn about the background of their new partners.

Job Prospects

Intense competition for jobs can be expected because private detective and investigator careers attract many qualified people, including relatively young retirees from law enforcement and the military.

The best job opportunities will be for entry-level positions in detective agencies. Candidates with related work experience and academic credentials, as well as those with strong interviewing skills and familiarity with internet research and computer systems, may find more job opportunities than others.

Salary Range

According to the U.S. Department of Labor Occupational Outlook Handbook, the 2021 median annual wage for private detectives and investigators was $59,380 annually, $28.55 per hour. The median wage is when half the workers in an occupation earn more than that amount, and half earn less. The lowest 10 percent earned less than $30,390, and the highest 10 percent earned more than $89,760.

In May 2021, the median annual wages for private detectives and investigators in the top industries in which they worked were as follows:

• Finance and insurance, $64,010

• Government, $62,090

• Investigation, guard, and armored car services, $51,630

Private detectives and investigators often work irregular hours because they conduct surveillance and contact people outside of regular work hours. They may work early mornings, evenings, weekends, and holidays. Also, they may have to work outdoors or from a vehicle, in all kinds of weather, depending on the purpose of the investigation.

Source of salary information: Bureau of Labor Statistics, U.S. Department of Labor, Occupational Outlook Handbook, 2021

Edition, Private Detectives, and Investigators at

https://www.bls.gov/ooh/protective-service/private-detectives-and-investigators.htm.

Typical Work Environment

Private detectives and investigators work in many different environments, depending on the type of case. Some may spend more time in offices, performing online research, computer database searches, and phone calls. Others spend more time "in the field," conducting interviews or surveillance.

Although investigators often work alone, some work with others as a team while conducting surveillance or carrying out large, complicated assignments.

Some of the work can involve confrontation, and some situations may require the investigator to carry a weapon. In most cases, however, a gun is not necessary because private detectives and investigators' purpose is to gather information, not to enforce laws or apprehend criminals.

Private detectives and investigators may work with demanding and sometimes distraught clients.

Chapter 3: Education Requirements

Education requirements for private investigators range from a high school diploma to a college degree. The minimum requirement is usually a high school diploma. However, an increasing number of states require applicants to complete at least one or two years of college coursework or have an associate's degree in a relevant field, such as criminal justice.

Degree Programs

Obtaining a formal degree at an accredited institution is one of the best ways to build a solid educational foundation for a career in private investigations.

Following are examples of degrees that would benefit a private investigator:

Criminal Justice Degree – The term "criminal justice" refers to the police, courts, and corrections as a system for administering city, county, state, and federal laws. The primary focus of this program is the justice system itself. The juvenile or adult accused of conduct that violates the law will be affected by law enforcement, prosecutorial, judicial, and correctional agencies.

The requirements of degree programs in this department stress an integrated view of the criminal justice system. In this view, all system components interrelate with all other components to provide coordinated justice administration. The criminal justice curriculum is designed to give students an understanding of the developing theoretical knowledge base in this field of study while providing an understanding of how each part relates.

Criminology is the scientific study of crime causes, consequences, prevention, and control. Knowledge gained from the scientific study of crime and criminal justice is the foundation for public policies and programs that improve the quality of life and promote social justice. Graduates of criminology programs are well-prepared for careers in law enforcement, criminal investigation, corrections, and probation.

Police Science - Police science bachelor's degree programs involve coursework in ethics, police leadership, diversity, and policing technologies. Additional specializations are sometimes available in areas such as forensics or security management.

To understand the education requirements for your state, start by visiting the licensing authority's website.

Continuing Education

Keeping your skills sharp and aligned with current methods and techniques is essential.

Industry Associations and Conferences - Private investigation industry conferences offer opportunities to learn about the latest investigative techniques, network with other investigators, and demonstrate the latest software and gadgets.

Self-Study Programs - Self-study programs are available for those who prefer to learn at their own pace without attending in-person classes. Such programs offer learning opportunities for aspiring investigators and seasoned professionals alike. Experienced private investigators can use such programs to learn about new areas of investigation.

Examination Requirements

Some states require applicants to pass an examination to measure knowledge and competence in the investigation field. Primarily, these exams will test your knowledge of investigations. Also, they may include questions about state laws and regulations on private investigators. The exams vary by state, so check the licensing authority's website for information on the specific examination requirements in your state.

Chapter 4: Training Requirements

The amount of training required to become a private investigator also varies widely from state to state. Some states don't have any requirements, while others require formal education, experience in a related field, or both. Some states with education requirements allow previous work experience to be substituted for education and vice versa. To understand the requirements for your state, start by visiting your state's licensing authority's website.

Prior Experience

Many states require that applicants have a certain number of years (or hours) of relevant experience.

For example, in California, prior experience in jobs such as the following may be considered as prior experience:

• A sworn law enforcement officer
• Military police officer
• Insurance adjuster
• An employee of a licensed PI or licensed repossessor
• Arson investigator for a public fire suppression agency
• An investigator for the public defender's office

Private Investigator Training Programs

Many reputable programs offer training specifically on private investigations. Following is a **sample** of programs that are currently available. Please note that these are examples of what is available and do not constitute an endorsement, nor is this an exhaustive list. Please take the time to evaluate each company, its curriculum, pricing structure, and online reviews before committing to a particular training program.

Blue Ribbon Investigative Institute

The Blue Ribbon Investigative Institute is licensed by the Florida Commission for Independent Education and certified by the Florida Department of Agriculture and the Department of Education to provide the 40-hour private investigator intern course required by the state. The course is written and taught by an actual private investigator. The course covers:

• The applicable state statutes and administrative code
• Professional ethics and legal issues
• How to interview witnesses and verify the truth
• How to use computers in the investigation process and sources of information
• Restrictions on records
• How to write reports
• How to find people
• Evidence
• Courtrooms, trials, and formal hearings
• Testifying as a witness
• Executive Protection

A certificate is provided upon completion of the course with a passing grade. The certificate must be submitted to the state with the license application form. To learn more about the Blue Ribbon Investigative Institute, visit their website at http://www.blueribboninvestigativeinst.com/.

Detective Training Institute

The Detective Training Institute offers a State-approved home study course to become a Qualified Private Investigator. The Private Investigator Course trains you on how to become a PI, and the latest investigative techniques, including state-of-the-art computer online investigative strategies. Other topics covered include

- Background Investigation and Research,
- Tracking and Locating Missing Persons
- Surveillance
- Legal Investigations
- Business Crimes Investigations,
- Starting Your New Career as a Private Eye

You can now begin your private investigator's education and development via home study or online.

No previous experience is required to get started in this exciting profession. Whether this is your first career or a career change, DTI makes it simple. The course provides detailed, step-by-step explanations with hundreds of photographs, making learning easy and fun.

And most importantly, you can learn private investigation from home in your spare time, on your schedule.

Enroll online or via mail. Online counseling is available, and students can send their exams for grading via fax or online. Private Investigator and Detective Training School is a specialized private investigation school licensed by the Nevada Commission on Post-secondary Education. Most students can complete this state-approved online program within ten weeks.

I recommend downloading and reading the first lesson, accessible on DTI's website. This will give you an idea of the high-quality information you'll receive via this excellent private eye training program.

To learn more about the Detective Training Institute, visit their website at http://www.detectivetraining.com/.

Discovery Detective Academy

The Discovery Detective Academy offers Investigations, Process Serving, and Security courses. Their Master's Course in investigations prepares you to run your agency. The course covers:

• Law: Civil, Criminal, Federal, and ethics
• Civil and criminal investigative techniques

- How to collect evidence and process a crime scene
- Forensics: handwriting analysis, fingerprints, lab results
- Document research and retrieval
- How to locate people, skip tracing
- Photography and videos
- Interrogation techniques
- Courtroom testimony
- How to manage cases
- How to set up and market your business

To learn more, visit their website at
https://www.discoverycollege.education/pi-master-course.html.

PIEducation

PIEducation is an internet-based private eye education service provider for the Private Security Industry. They offer courses primarily to private investigators that require continuing education as a part of their license renewal. Several states have approved these courses as online continuing education.

Following are examples of PIEducation continuing education courses:

- Surveillance learning
- Death investigations
- Forensic photography
- Interviewing witness
- Bounty hunting training

- Private investigation laws and ethics
- Skip Tracing

To learn more about the courses offered by PIEducation, visit their website at https://pieducation.com/.

Private Investigator Training and Security Training Program

With this program, you can train at home to be a private investigator, detective, or security specialist or to work in personal or executive protection and intelligence and investigations with these online courses and distance learning diploma programs from accredited institutions.

To learn more, visit their website at https://www.worldwidelearn.com/career-training/private-investigator.htm.

Rasmussen College - Criminal Justice Program

The Rasmussen College criminal justice program offers a career that allows you to have a direct positive impact on individuals, businesses, and entire communities. You can choose from various criminal justice specialties, including law enforcement, corrections, psychology, and homeland security.

- Learn from current sheriffs, sergeants, and other seasoned law enforcement professionals

• Gain real-world insight through police ride-along, correctional visits, and other hands-on opportunities

• Examine the social and behavioral issues involved in the study of crime to help you in the field

For more information, visit the website at http://www.rasmussen.edu/degrees/justice-studies/criminal-justice/ or contact:

Michael Schwartz

Rasmussen College

Address: 8300 Norman Center Drive, Suite 300

Phone: 952-806-3900

FAX: 952-831-0624

Michael.Schwartz@rasmussen.edu

The Stratford Career Institute

The Stratford Career Institute offers a Private Investigator Training Distance Learning Course (home study) that provides fundamental instruction on critical areas such as

• Ethics and legal issues

• Various types of investigations, including accidents, criminal, domestic, fraud, financial, insurance, missing persons, and undercover work

• Resources, tools, and techniques in the P.I.'s toolbox

• How to interview witnesses

• How to provide testimony

• How to conduct research

To learn more, visit their website at

https://www.scitraining.com/private-investigator.

Firearms Training

Firearms are not required for private investigation work, but many licensed private eyes carry one for personal safety. Most states require a valid firearm permit issued by the appropriate agency. Also, some states require private investigator applicants to submit separate firearms permit applications, and some require applicants to complete a formal firearms training course with an approved instructor. Please check with the individual state licensing agency to determine their specific requirements.

On-the-Job Training

Probably the most effective training method is to learn on the job from an experienced private investigator. In some states, an aspiring private investigator must work in an apprentice role for a specific period. This allows the individual to get valuable on-the-job training from experienced investigators.

Check the licensing authority's website for information on the specific training requirements in your state.

Chapter 5: Overview of State Licensing Requirements

This section provides a state-by-state overview of private investigator license requirements. Each state overview provides:

• The licensing authority that is responsible for issuing licenses

• Contact information, including the name, address, phone number, and fax number

• Email address (if available)

• Website URL

• Link to the state law governing private investigator licensing (if available)

• Details on the general requirements. Please note that many states have detailed requirements that are modified periodically. I recommend you visit the state licensing website for a more detailed and current list of requirements.

Licensing requirements, eligibility criteria, application processes, and fees vary by state, and those requirements may change as new legislation is passed. To obtain the most up-to-date information and application forms, please contact the state licensing authority using the contact information listed. The state licensing website provides state-specific information on

- State licensing requirements

- Eligibility guidelines

- Minimum age, citizenship, and residency requirements

- Forms necessary to apply for or renew a license

- Firearm training and licensing requirements

- Fees

Additional Requirements

In addition to obtaining a private investigator's license, some states may have additional requirements on:

- Education/training

- Experience

- Examinations

- Business license

- Firearms licensing and training

- Insurance

- Fingerprinting

- Background checks

Typical Reasons for Application Denial

The following are examples of some common reasons for an application being denied. Reasons vary by state, so check the requirements for the specific state you plan to apply to.

- Not meeting the minimum age requirement

- Prior felony conviction

- Prior misdemeanor conviction

- Currently under indictment

- Found incompetent due to a mental defect or disease by a court

- Registered as a sex offender

- Dishonorably discharged from the U.S. military

- Not having a physical location in the state

- Engaging in the private investigation profession without a license

- Previously had a private investigator license revoked

- Suffer from narcotics addiction or dependence or habitual drunkenness

Reciprocity Agreements

Some states have reciprocity agreements that allow P.I.s to do investigative work in both states. California, Florida, Georgia, Louisiana, North Carolina, Oklahoma, Tennessee, and Virginia have reciprocity agreements. These agreements are subject to change, so please check with the appropriate agency to verify their current status.

Other Uses for State Licensing Websites

In addition to providing information on obtaining your private investigator's license, state websites also provide the following:

• Overview of requirements and process to renew an existing license
• How to update your contact information
• How to verify credentials for an existing licensee
• View state laws that govern private detectives in the state
• Copies of state laws that govern private investigator licensing and activities

Important Note:

Licensing requirements, eligibility criteria, application processes, and fees vary by state. To obtain the most up-to-date information and application forms, please contact the state licensing authority using the contact information listed.

Chapter 6: Licensing Requirements by State

Alabama

Licensing Authority

Until recently, private investigators were not required to be licensed in the state of Alabama. In 2013, the Alabama legislature introduced Senate Bill 172. There was nearly unanimous support for the bill in both the House and Senate. Bill 172 was sponsored by Senator Bill Holtzclaw of Madison, Alabama, and Representative Howard Sanderford from Huntsville, Alabama.

Contact Information

Alabama Private Investigation Board (APIB)

P.O. Box 241206

Montgomery, AL 36124-1206

Phone Number 334-215-0693

Fax 334-274-0684

Email: apib@leadership-alliance.org

Website: http://www.apib.alabama.gov/

View the Alabama Private Investigation Regulatory Act:
http://www.apib.alabama.gov/PDF/law/CHAPTER_25B.pdf

General Requirements

The following is general licensing information. Please visit the website above for specific licensing information, application forms, insurance requirements, fees, and special licensing requirements.

Minimum Requirements

To apply for a private investigator license in the state of Alabama, applicants must:

• Be at least 21 years of age

• Have not been declared by any court of competent jurisdiction incompetent because of mental defect or disease (unless a court of competent jurisdiction has subsequently declared the applicant competent)

• Have not been convicted of a crime of moral turpitude (with the Board having final determination on the interpretation of moral turpitude)

• Have not been convicted of a felony crime

• Pass an examination by the Board designed to measure knowledge and competence in the investigation field, OR (a) Be an investigator holding a current business license in the state of Alabama on the effective date of the adoption of the rules and regulations of the Board

• The opportunity to apply for a private investigator license issued under this rule shall expire 365 days after the implementation of the rules and regulations of the Board. Holders of these licenses shall be eligible to renew their licenses, as are any other licensed private investigators

Note: Soon, private investigators will be required to submit their fingerprints and undergo background checks. They must also complete continuing education courses like private eyes in many other states. Check the Alabama website for the most up-to-date requirements.

Alaska

As of the date this ebook was published, a private investigator's license is not required in the State of Alaska. Some individual cities in Alaska, such as Anchorage and Fairbanks, have licensing requirements.

Visit the state website at http://alaska.gov/ for the most up-to-date information.

Arizona

Licensing Authority

The Arizona Department of Public Safety Licensing Unit is responsible for private investigator licensing in Arizona.

Contact Information

Arizona Department of Public Safety
Licensing Unit
PO Box 6328, MD 1160
Phoenix, AZ 85005
Phone: (602) 223-2361
Fax: (602) 223-2938

Website: https://www.azdps.gov/services/public/licensing

General Requirements

The following is general licensing information. Please visit the website above for specific licensing information, application forms, insurance requirements, fees, and special licensing requirements.

To apply for a private investigator license in the state of Arizona, applicants must:

• Be at least 18 years old

• Be a U.S. citizen or legal resident

• Have no felony convictions

• Not be under indictment for a felony

• Not be a registered sex offender

• Not be on parole or probation

• Have no misdemeanor convictions for violent acts, fraud, theft, domestic violence, sexual misconduct, or narcotics violations in the last five years. This holds even if the conviction was set aside.

• Have never been convicted of attempting to act as a PI without a license

Arkansas

Licensing Authority

The Arkansas State Police Regulatory Services Division is responsible for the oversight and licensing of private investigators and private security companies.

Contact Information

Arkansas State Police
One State Police Plaza Dr., Little Rock, AR 72209
Phone Number: 501-618-8000

Website: https://www.azdps.gov/licensing/pi

Minimum Requirements

General Requirements

The following is general licensing information. Please visit the website for specific licensing information, application forms, insurance, fees, and special licensing requirements.

In addition to two years of work experience alongside a licensed PI and passing the state board exam, applicants must meet the following additional requirements:

- U.S. Citizen or legal resident
- No felony or Class A misdemeanor convictions
- No history of violent or immoral behavior

• Successfully pass a background check

• Be fingerprinted

Note: The state reciprocates on private investigator licenses with the following states: Tennessee, Louisiana, and Oklahoma. To qualify for reciprocity, the license must be current, and the applicant must have been licensed in the reciprocal state for at least two consecutive years.

California

Licensing Authority

Private investigator licensing in California is handled by the Department of Consumer Affairs, Bureau of Security and Investigative Services.

Contact Information

Physical Address: 2420 Del Paso Rd., Ste. 270, Sacramento, CA 95834

Licensing Address: P.O. Box 989002, West Sacramento, CA 95798

Phone: (916) 322-4000 or (800) 952-5210

Fax: (916) 575-7290

Website: http://www.bsis.ca.gov/forms_pubs/pi_fact.shtml

General Requirements

The following is general licensing information. Please visit the website for specific licensing information, application forms, insurance requirements, fees, and special licensing requirements.

• Be 18 or older.

• Undergo a criminal history background check through the California Department of Justice (DOJ) and the Federal Bureau of Investigation (FBI).

• Have at least three years (2,000 hours each year, totaling 6,000 hours) of compensated experience in investigative work; or

• Have a law degree or completed a four-year course in police science plus two years (4,000 hours) of experience; or

• Have an associate's degree in police science, criminal law, or justice and two and a half years (5,000 hours) of experience.

• Experience must be certified by your employer and have been received while you were employed as a sworn law enforcement officer, military police officer, insurance adjuster, an employee of a licensed PI or licensed repossessor, an arson investigator for a public fire suppression agency, or an investigator for the public defender's office. (Work as a process server, public records researcher, custodial attendant for a law enforcement agency, bailiff, an agent who collects debts in writing or by telephone after the debtor has been located, or a person who repossesses property after it has been located is not considered qualifying experience).

• Pass a two-hour multiple-choice examination covering laws and regulations, terminology, civil and criminal liability, evidence handling, undercover investigations, and surveillance. A copy of the Private Investigator Act will be sent to you.

Upon notification that you have passed the examination, you must submit a licensing fee to the Bureau of Security and Investigative Services, P.O. Box 989002, West Sacramento, CA 95798-9002.

Please see the website listed above for information on the current fee amount.

Colorado

Licensing Authority

Private investigator licensing in Colorado is governed by the Colorado Department of Regulatory Agencies, Office of Private Investigator Licensure.

Contact Information

Office of Private Investigator Licensure
1560 Broadway, Suite 1350
Denver, CO 80202
Phone: 303-894-7800
Fax: 303-894-2310

Email: dora_privateinvestigators@state.co.us

Website: https://dpo.colorado.gov/PrivateInvestigator

The Colorado Office of Private Investigator Licensure website has helpful information such as

- Applications and forms
- Renew your existing license
- The Private Investigator's Practice Act
- Private Investigator Rules and Regulations
- Other resources

Connecticut

Licensing Authority

The Connecticut Department of Emergency Services and Public Protection is responsible for processing license applications and employee registrations, as well as investigating complaints concerning violations of the license statutes.

Contact Information

Connecticut State Police
Special Licensing & Firearms Unit
1111 Country Club Rd.
Middletown, CT 06457

Website: https://portal.ct.gov/DESPP

General Requirements

The following is general licensing information. Please visit the website for specific licensing information, application forms, insurance, fees, and special licensing requirements.

• Applicants for a Private Detective License must be

• At least 25 years of age

• Have a good moral character

• Have at least five years of full-time experience as a licensed private detective, or five years of full-time experience as a registered Private Investigator, five years full-time experience operating a Proprietary Detective Agency, or five years full-time experience as an investigator with any federal state or local government, or five years full-time experience as a Detective with a federal, state or local police department or, Any other recognized five years full-time industry-related investigative experience or have had at least ten years of experience as a police officer with a federal, state or organized municipal police department.

• If the applicant is a corporation, association, or partnership, the person filing on behalf of the business must meet all the qualifications detailed above and shall be an officer of such corporation or member of such association or partnership.

The commissioner may, at his discretion, substitute up to one year of experience for a private detective license applicant upon proof of satisfactory participation in a course of instruction pertinent to the license.

Employment as a security officer does not qualify as time earned to obtain a private detective license.

No license will be issued to any person who has been:

• Convicted of any felony

• Convicted of any misdemeanor, or equivalent conviction in another jurisdiction, within the past seven years

• Convicted of any offense involving moral turpitude, or

• Discharged from military service under conditions that demonstrate questionable moral character

Delaware

Licensing Authority

The Delaware State Police is responsible for regulating private investigative and security agencies, alarm companies, constables, bail enforcement agents, etc. The Delaware State Police defines a private investigator as "any person who engages in the business or accepts employment to obtain or furnish information to conduct investigations.

The Delaware State Police website describes the licensing application process, the fees required, a list of helpful FAQs, and the criteria for obtaining a private investigator license. The website is the best place to go to get information, forms, contact information, etc.

Contact Information

Delaware State Police
Blue Hen Corporate Center
655 South Bay Road, Suite 1B
Dover, DE 19901
PHONE: 302-739-5991
FAX: 302-739-5888

Website: https://dsp.delaware.gov/professional-licensing/

General Requirements

The following is general licensing information. Please visit the website for specific licensing information, application forms, insurance requirements, fees, and special licensing requirements.

The Process to Get a Private Investigator License in Delaware

Before beginning the application process, please note that applicants must be 21 years or older and working for a licensed private investigation agency in the State of Delaware. The process to get a private investigator license in Delaware is as follows:

1. Get Fingerprints and Pictures

First, visit one of the following locations to get fingerprinted and have your picture taken:

State Bureau of Identification655 South Bay Road, Suite 1B, Dover, DE 19901

The Delaware State Bureau of Identification is open Monday through Friday from 8:30 AM to 3:30 PM. No appointment is necessary.

Delaware State Police: Troop 2

100 Lagrange Ave, Newark, DE 19702

This location is available by appointment only. To schedule an appointment, call 302-739-2528.

2. Complete and Submit an Application

Next, complete and submit the application. You can also pick up a physical copy of the application at the two locations listed above.

3. Pay the Application Fee

Pay the non-refundable application fee of $85.00. You can pay the licensing application fee in cash, certified check, Visa, Master Card, Discover, company check, or money order. The DSP does not accept personal checks or American Express credit cards.

Additional Information

The application process to get a private investigator license in Delaware takes at least two weeks to process. If and when your application is approved, ID cards will be mailed to the address listed on your application.

If you need to contact the Special Licensing section of the DSP for any reason, their contact information is as follows:

Email address:
DSP_SBIDETECTIVELICENSINGMAIL@STATE.DE.US

Phone: 302-739-5991
Fax: 302-739-5888

Mailing Address:

Professional Licensing Section, P.O. Box 430, Dover, DE 19903

Reciprocity

Delaware does not have reciprocity agreements with any other states. If you plan to work as a private investigator in the state, you need to apply for a Delaware license.

Florida

Licensing Authority

The Department of Agriculture and Consumer Services, Division of Licensing, licenses and regulates the private investigative industry per Chapter 493 of Florida's state statutes.

Contact Information

Florida Department of Agriculture and Consumer Services
P.O. Box 5767
Tallahassee, FL 32314-5767
1-800-HELP-FLA (1-800-435-7352)

Website: https://www.fdacs.gov/Business-Services/Private-Investigation-Licenses

General Requirements

The following is general licensing information. Please visit the website listed above for specific licensing information, application forms, insurance requirements, fees, and any special licensing requirements.

• Be at least 18 years old

• Be a U.S. citizen or legal resident

• Have no disqualifying criminal history

• Be of good moral character

• Have no history of mental illness

• Have no history of use of illegal drugs

• Have no history of alcoholism

• Have two years of experience (which can be gained through first obtaining a Class CC Private Investigator Intern License)

Georgia

Licensing Authority

Private Investigator licensing in Georgia is handled by the Secretary of State Georgia Board of Private Detectives and Security Agencies. The Board administers The Private Detective & Security Agencies Act" to safeguard this state's citizens by regulating private detective and security businesses. The Board consists of seven members appointed by the Governor. The Board has the authority to determine applicants' qualifications for licensure, investigate complaints, and take appropriate disciplinary action.

Contact Information

Georgia Board of Private Detectives and Security Agencies
214 State Capitol
Atlanta, Georgia 30334
404.656.2881

Website: https://sos.ga.gov/board-private-detectives-and-security-agencies

General Requirements

The following is general licensing information. Please visit the website listed above for specific licensing information, application forms, insurance requirements, fees, and any special licensing requirements.

View this document for more detailed information:

https://sos.ga.gov/plb/acrobat/Laws/31_Priv_Detective_and_Secur
ity_43-38.pdf

• Licenses in Georgia are issued only to companies. The holder of
the company license must be an individual, the owner, a partner,
or an officer of the corporation or LLC who is qualified by
experience or education

• Two years of experience is required - either in law enforcement
or as a registered private detective employed by a licensed private
detective company. The education required is a four-year degree
from an accredited college or university in Criminal Justice or a
related field of study

• To be employed as an investigator with a licensed company, you
must be at least 18 years of age and must meet the minimum
requirements established by the Board

Reciprocity

Effective Friday, March 27, 2020, allows for Private Investigators
or Private Investigative agencies who are licensed in either state
and whose license(s) is/are in good standing in that state, to enter
the reciprocating state to conduct private investigations only if the
private investigation originated in their home state.

Furthermore, investigation in the reciprocating state is limited to
thirty (30) days per agency per case. Investigations exceeding

thirty days must be handled by a licensed private investigation agency in the reciprocating state. Please note that the exemption does not authorize private investigators or private investigative agencies to solicit private investigative business in the reciprocating state or conduct private investigative business in the reciprocating state other than as stated above.

The Georgia Board of Private Detective and Security Agencies currently has Limited License Recognition Agreements with the following states: Florida, Louisiana, North Carolina, Tennessee, Virginia, and Alabama.

Hawaii

Licensing Authority

Private Investigator licensing in Hawaii is handled by the Hawaii Department of Commerce and Consumer Affairs - Professional and Vocational Licensing, Board of Private Detectives and Guards.

Contact Information

DCCA-PVL

Attention: PDG

P.O. Box 3469

Honolulu, HI 96801

Telephone: (808) 586-2705

Email: detective@dcca.hawaii.gov

Website: http://cca.hawaii.gov/pvl/boards/private/

General Requirements

Please see https://cca.hawaii.gov/pvl/files/2013/06/Require-Instruct-App-for-Detective-or-Guard-Agency_12.16R.pdf for detailed requirements.

Idaho

Licensing Authority

Currently, there is no private investigator licensing requirement at the state level. Individual cities within the state, such as Boise, do have licensing requirements.

A business license and or insurance bond may be required. For information on obtaining a business license in Idaho, please visit https://www2.labor.idaho.gov/ibrs/ibr.aspx.

Illinois

Licensing Authority

Private investigator licensing in Illinois is handled by the Illinois Department of Financial and Professional Regulation, Division of Professional Regulation. The department issues licenses for private detective professions:

• Licensed Private Detective

• Licensed Private Detective Agency

• Licensed Private Detective Agency Branch Office

• Approved Training Course School

• Firearm Control Card (FCC)

• Permanent Employee Registration Card (PERC)

• Firearm Instructor

• Approved 20-Hour Basic Training Program

• Approved Basic 40-Hour Firearm Training Course

Contact Information

100 West Randolph, 9th Floor | Chicago, IL 60601
320 West Washington, 3rd Floor | Springfield, IL 62786
Phone: 1 (888) 473-4858
Website: http://www.idfpr.com/profs/Detective.asp

General Requirements

The following is general licensing information. Please visit the website listed above for specific licensing information, application forms, insurance requirements, fees, and any special licensing requirements.

You must also be able to meet the following minimum requirements to be eligible for private investigator jobs in Illinois:

• Be at least 21 years old

• Either no felony convictions or ten years have passed since your sentence was completed

• Is not a registered sex offender

• Must be of good moral character

• Be psychologically and physically fit for the duties of a private detective

• Have no narcotic or alcohol addictions

Please visit the website listed above for a complete list of requirements and to learn the steps involved in the application process.

Indiana

Licensing Authority

The Indiana Professional Licensing Agency, Private Investigator & Security Guard Licensing Board handles private investigator licensing in Indiana.

Contact Information

Indiana Professional Licensing Agency

Attn: Private Investigator & Security Guard Licensing Board

402 W Washington Street, Room W072

Staff Phone Number: (317) 234-3022

Staff Fax Number: (317) 233-4236

Staff Email: pla10@pla.in.gov

Indianapolis, IN 46204

Website: http://www.in.gov/pla/pisg.htm

General Requirements

The following is general licensing information. Please visit the website listed above for specific licensing information, application forms, insurance requirements, fees, and any special licensing requirements.

• At least twenty-one (21) years of age

• Demonstrates the necessary knowledge and skills, as determined by the board, to conduct a private investigator firm competently

• The board may not issue a private investigator firm license to a business entity unless one officer, in the case of a corporation; or one partner, in the case of a partnership; meets the personal qualifications as set out in subsection (a) unless otherwise provided the board may deny a license unless the applicant makes a showing satisfactory to the board that the applicant or if the applicant is a business entity, the officer or partner

• Has not committed an act which, if committed by a licensee, would be grounds for the suspension or revocation of a license under this chapter;

• Has not been convicted of a felony or misdemeanor that has a direct bearing upon the applicant's ability to practice competently;

• Has not been refused a license under this chapter or had a license revoked;

• Has not, while unlicensed, committed or aided and abetted in the commission of an act for which a license is required by this chapter;

• Is not on probation or parole; and is not being sought under an active warrant against the applicant, officer, or partner.

Please visit the website for a complete list of requirements and to learn the steps involved in the application process.

Iowa

Licensing Authority

Private investigator licensing in Iowa is handled by the Iowa Department of Public Safety, Administrative Services Division.

Contact Information

Bail Enforcement/Private Investigative/Security Licensing Program Services Bureau

Administrative Services Division

Iowa Department of Public Safety

Department of Public Safety Building

215 East 7th Street, 4th Floor

Des Moines, IA 50319-0045

Telephone: (515) 725-6230

Fax: (515) 725-6264

Email: piinfo@dps.state.ia.us

Website: https://dps.iowa.gov/divisions/administrative-services/bail-enforcement-private-investigation-private-security

General Requirements

The following is general licensing information. Please visit the website for specific licensing information, application forms, insurance, fees, and special licensing requirements.

Applications for a license or license renewal shall be submitted to the commissioner in the form the commissioner prescribes. A license or license renewal shall not be issued unless the applicant:

• Is eighteen years of age or older

• Is not a peace officer

• Has never been convicted of a felony or aggravated misdemeanor

• Is not addicted to the use of alcohol or a controlled substance

• Does not have a history of repeated acts of violence

• Is of good moral character and has not been judged guilty of a crime involving moral turpitude

• Has not been convicted of a crime described in section 708.3, 708.4, 708.5, 708.6, 708.8, or 708.9 (visit the website at the address listed above for links to detailed legal codes)

• Has not been convicted of illegally using, carrying, or possessing a dangerous weapon

• Has not been convicted of fraud

• Provides fingerprints to the department. Note: The fingerprints may be submitted by the department to the federal bureau of investigation through the state criminal history repository for a national criminal history check

65

• Complies with other qualifications and requirements the commissioner adopts by rule

• If the applicant is a corporation, the requirements of subsection 1 apply to the president and to each officer, commissioner, or employee who is actively involved in the licensed business in Iowa

• If the applicant is a partnership or association, the requirements of subsection 1 apply to each partner or association member

• Each employee of an applicant or licensee shall possess the same qualifications required by subsection 1 for a licensee

Kansas

Licensing Authority

Since 1972, the Office of the Attorney General has been responsible for the licensing and regulation of private detectives and private detective agencies doing business in Kansas.

Contact Information

Private Detective Licensing Unit
120 SW 10th Ave., 2nd Floor
Topeka, KS 66612-1597
Phone: (785) 296-4240
Fax: (785) 368-6468

Email: ksagpi@ag.ks.gov

Website: http://ag.ks.gov/licensing/pi-licensing

General Requirements

The following is general licensing information. Please visit the website for specific licensing information, application forms, insurance, fees, and special licensing requirements.

Before an application for a license may be granted, the applicant or, if the applicant is an organization, all of the officers, directors, partners or associates shall:

• Be at least 21 years of age

• Be a citizen of the United States

• Be of good moral character

• Comply with such other qualifications as the attorney general adopts by rules and regulations

The Kansas attorney general may deny a license if the applicant has:

• Committed any act which, if committed by a licensee, would be grounds for the suspension or revocation of a license under this act

• Committed any act constituting dishonesty or fraud

• A bad moral character or a bad reputation for truth, honesty, and integrity

• Been convicted of a felony or, within 10 years immediately before the date of application, been convicted of any crime involving moral turpitude, dishonesty, vehicular homicide, assault, battery, assault of a law enforcement officer, misdemeanor battery against a law enforcement officer, criminal restraint, sexual battery, endangering a child, intimidation of a witness or victim or illegally using, carrying, or possessing a dangerous weapon;

• Been refused a license under this act or had a license suspended or revoked in this state or any other jurisdiction or had a license censured, limited, or conditioned two or more times in this state or any other jurisdiction;

• Been an officer, director, partner, or associate of any person who has been refused a license under this act or whose license has been suspended or revoked in this state or any other jurisdiction or had a license censured, limited, or conditioned two or more times in this state or any other jurisdiction;

• While unlicensed committed or aided and abetted the commission of any act for which a license is required by this act; or

• Knowingly made any false statement in the application

The attorney general may charge a fee for initial application forms and materials in an amount fixed by the attorney general. The fee shall be credited against the application fee of any person who subsequently submits an application

Please visit the website listed above for a complete list of requirements, and current fees, and to learn the steps involved in the application process.

Kentucky

Licensing Authority

Private investigator licensing in Kentucky is handled by the Kentucky Board of Licensure for Private Investigators. The Board serves to promote, preserve, and protect public safety and welfare through effective regulation of the practice of private investigations. The Board this mission through the examination, testing, and licensing of prospective private investigators; regulation and discipline of all licensed private investigators; and through appropriate communication of information and laws about the practice of private investigations in Kentucky.

Contact Information

Kentucky Board of Licensure for Private Investigators
911 Leawood Drive
Frankfort, KY 40601
Telephone: 502-782-8809
Fax: 502-696-4961

Email: Sandy.Deaton@Ky.Gov

Website: http://kpi.ky.gov/

Minimum Requirements

• Must be at least 21 years old

• Be of good moral character

• Be a U.S. citizen or lawful resident alien

• If you have any felony convictions, ten years must have passed since the completion of your sentence

• No convictions for crimes involving dishonesty or moral turpitude within the past five years

• If you are a military veteran you must not have been dishonorably discharged

• Be of sound mental capacity

• No misdemeanor or higher convictions within the past three years for crimes involving controlled substances

• May not have been enrolled in a facility or program for substance abuse in the past three years

• May not chronically or habitually use alcohol or drugs

Louisiana

Licensing Authority

Private investigator licensing in the state of Louisiana is handled by the Louisiana State Board of Private Investigators Examiners.

Contact Information

Louisiana State Board of Private Investigators Examiners
7414 Perkins Rd.
Suite #120
Baton Rouge, LA 70808
Phone: 1-800-299-9696 or 225-763-3556
Fax: 225-763-353

Website: http://lsbpie.com/

General Requirements

The following is general licensing information. Please visit the website listed above for specific licensing information, application forms, insurance requirements, fees, and any special licensing requirements.

• Is of legal age (18)

• Is a citizen of the United States or a resident alien holding proper documentation to • work in the United States

• Has not been convicted in any jurisdiction of any felony or a crime involving moral turpitude

• Has not been declared by any court of competent jurisdiction to be incompetent because of a mental defect or disease which has not been restored

• Is not a practicing alcoholic or drug addict

• If a corporation, shall be incorporated under the laws of this state or shall be duly qualified to do business within this state with a valid certificate of authority issued by the Secretary of State, and shall have an agent for service of process designated as required by law

• If in the discretion of the Board, the applicant provides inadequate information to allow the Board to ascertain whether the applicant satisfied the qualifications for licensure, the applicant shall be required to provide additional information for the application or may be required to present himself/herself for an interview for this purpose

• A "Private investigation agency license" issued to any person or entity, as defined in RS 37:3503 (8), where the individual seeking license or the partner of the partnership seeking licensure, or the principal corporate officer of the corporation seeking license (visit the website listed above for more detailed information on legal codes and statutes)

• Has at least three years of experience within the last ten years either working as a private investigator or in an investigative capacity

• Satisfies all other requirements for licensing

Maine

Licensing Authority

Private investigator licensing in Maine is handled by the Maine State Police Licensing Division. The Maine State Police Licensing Division also licenses professional investigators, investigative assistants, and Professional security companies.

Contact Information

Maine State Police
State House Station 164
Augusta, ME. 04333
Phone (207) 624-7210
Fax (207) 287-3424

Commanding Officer, Lt. Scott W. Ireland
Scott.W.Ireland@maine.gov

Website: https://www.maine.gov/dps/msp/licenses-permits/professional-investigator

See also, the Maine State Law governing private investigators.

General Requirements

The following is general licensing information. Please visit the website listed above for specific licensing information, application forms, insurance requirements, fees, and any special licensing requirements.

A person is qualified to be licensed as a professional investigator who:

• Is at least 21 years of age

• Is a citizen or resident alien of the United States

• Is a graduate of an accredited high school or has been granted high school equivalency status by the State

• Has demonstrated good moral character and has not been convicted of a crime that is punishable by a maximum term of imprisonment equal to or exceeding one year, or a crime enumerated in this chapter. The determination of good moral character must be made in writing, based upon evidence recorded by a governmental entity. The chief shall consider matters recorded within the previous five years, including, but not limited to, the following:

• Records of incidents of abuse by the applicant of family or household members provided according to Title 19-A, section 4012, subsection 1;

• Records provided by the Department of Health and Human Services regarding the failure of the applicant to meet child or family support obligations;

• Records of three or more convictions of the applicant for Class D or E crimes;

• Records of three or more civil violations by the applicant; or

• Records that the applicant has engaged in recklessness or negligence that endangered the safety of others, including the use of weapons or motor vehicles;

Maryland

Licensing Authority

Private Investigator Licensing in the State of Maryland is handled by the Maryland State Police, Licensing Division. The Licensing Division is responsible for administering the law and conducting investigations concerning the licensing of Private Detectives, Private Detective Agencies, Security Guards and Security Guard Agencies, Security Systems Technicians, and Security Systems Agencies.

Contact Information

Maryland State Police
Licensing Division
1111 Reisterstown Road
Pikesville, MD 21208
Attn.: Private Detective Unit

Website:

http://mdsp.maryland.gov/Organization/Pages/CriminalInvestigatio nBureau/LicensingDivision/ProfessionalLicenses/PrivateDetective Agencies.aspx

General Requirements

The following is general licensing information. Please visit the website listed above for specific licensing information, application

forms, insurance requirements, fees, and any special licensing requirements.

An applicant may be either an individual or a firm. An individual shall be of good character and reputation. If the applicant is a firm, each member shall have good character and reputation. The individual or firm representative shall be at least 25 years old. All applicants shall meet the required experience outlined below:

• At least five years of experience as a full-time certified or licensed private detective; OR

• At least five years of experience as a full-time police officer with an organized police agency, and completed successfully a police officer training course that is recognized and approved by the Maryland Police Training Commission; OR

• At least three years of experience in an investigative capacity as a detective while serving as a police officer with an organized police agency; OR

• At least: three years of experience in an investigative capacity in any unit of the United States, of the State, or a county or municipal corporation of the State for law enforcement; and completed successfully the police officer training required by the Maryland Police Training Commission; OR

• At least five years of experience as a full-time fire investigator for a fire department or law enforcement agency of the State or a county or municipal corporation of the State; and completed successfully the training certified by the Maryland Police Training Commission or the Maryland Fire-Rescue Education and Training Commission.

Massachusetts

Licensing Authority

The Massachusetts State Police Certification Unit handles private investigator licensing in Massachusetts.

Contact Information

Massachusetts State Police

470 Worcester Road, Framingham, MA 01702

Phone: (508) 820-2300

Fax: (617) 727-6874 or (508) 879-694

Website:

https://www.mass.gov/service-details/requirements-for-a-private-investigator-license

General Requirements

The following is general licensing information. Please visit the website listed above for specific licensing information, application forms, insurance requirements, fees, and any special licensing requirements.

An application for a license to engage in the private detective business or a license to engage in the business of watch, guard, or patrol agency shall be filed with the colonel of the state police on forms furnished by him, and statements of fact therein shall be under oath of the applicant.

The application shall include a certification by each of three reputable citizens of the commonwealth residing in the community in which the applicant resides or has a place of business or in which the applicant proposes to conduct his business, that he has personally known the applicant for at least three years, that he has read the application and believes each of the statements made therein to be true, that he is not related to the applicant by blood or marriage, and that the applicant is honest and of good moral character.

The applicant, or its resident manager, superintendent, or official representative, shall be of good moral character if the applicant is a corporation.

The applicant shall have been regularly employed for not less than three years as a detective doing investigating work, a former member of an investigative service of the United States, a former police officer of rank or grade higher than that of patrolman of the commonwealth, any political subdivision thereof or an official police department of another state, or a police officer in good standing formerly employed for not less than ten years with the commonwealth, or any political subdivision thereof or with an official police department of another state.

A license will not be granted to anyone convicted in any state of the United States of a felony. No person convicted of violating section ninety-nine or ninety-nine A of chapter two hundred and seventy-two of the general laws shall be granted a license, and any license previously granted to such person shall be revoked.

Michigan

Licensing Authority

In Michigan, a license is required when furnishing, for hire, fee or reward, professional investigator or private detective services, including locating individuals and investigating damage or crimes.

Contact Information

Corporations, Securities & Commercial Licensing
Licensing Division
PO Box 30018
Lansing, MI 48909
Phone: (517) 241-9221
Fax: (517) 373-2162
Website: http://www.michigan.gov/pi

General Requirements

The following is general licensing information. Please visit the website listed above for specific licensing information, application forms, insurance requirements, fees, and any special licensing requirements.

• A licensed professional investigator must meet the following requirements:

• Is a citizen of the United States

• Is not less than 25 years of age

• Has a high school education or its equivalent

• Has not been convicted of a felony, or a misdemeanor involving any of the following:

• Dishonesty or fraud

• Unauthorized divulging or selling of information or evidence

• Impersonation of a law enforcement officer or employee of the United States or a state, or a political subdivision of the United States or a state

• Illegally using, carrying, or possessing a dangerous weapon

• Two or more alcohol-related offenses

• Controlled substances as defined under the Michigan Public Health Code

• Has not been dishonorably discharged from a branch of the United States military service

For not less than three years has been or is any of the following on a full-time basis:

• Lawfully engaged in the professional investigation business as a licensee, registrant, or investigative employee in another state

• Lawfully engaged in the investigation business as an investigative employee of the holder of a license to conduct a professional investigation agency

• An investigator, detective, special agent, intelligence specialist, parole agent, probation officer, or certified police officer employed by any government executive, military, judicial, or legislative agency, or other public authority engaged in investigative or intelligence activities

• A graduate of an accredited institution of higher education with a baccalaureate or postgraduate degree in the field of police administration, security management, investigation, law, criminal justice, or computer forensics certificate study that is acceptable to the department

• Lawfully engaged in the investigation business as a full-time proprietary or in-house investigator employed by a business or attorney, or as an investigative reporter employed by a recognized media outlet, acceptable to the department

• Has posted a $10,000.00 bond or insurance policy provided for in this act.

In the case of a person, firm, partnership, company, limited liability company, or corporation now doing or seeking to do business in this state, the manager shall comply with the qualifications of this section.

Minnesota

Licensing Authority

Private Investigator Licensing in Minnesota is handled by the State of Minnesota Board of Private Detective and Protective Agent Services. The mission of the Private Detective and Protective Agent Services Board is to ensure investigative and security service practitioners meet statutory qualifications and training for licensure and maintain standards outlined in Minnesota Statutes and Administrative Rules.

Contact Information

The State of Minnesota Board of Private Detective and Protective Agent Services
1430 Maryland Avenue East
St. Paul, MN 55106
Phone: (651) 793-2666
Fax: (651) 793-7065
TTYL: (651) 282-6555

Email: mn.pdb@state.mn.us

Website: https://dps.mn.gov/entity/pdb/Pages/default.aspx

See also, the Minnesota State Law.

General Requirements

The following is general licensing information. Please visit the website listed above for specific licensing information, application forms, insurance requirements, fees, and any special licensing requirements.

Listed below are some of the basic requirements for all applicants (including Qualified Representatives, Minnesota Managers, and all parties required to sign the application form):

• Each person signing the application must be at least 18 years of age

• Each person must have a record that is free of felony convictions and no record of convictions of offenses identified in the statute

• A $10,000 Surety Bond (private detective or protective agent) at the time of application

• Acceptable Proof of Financial Responsibility documentation

• Complete required application materials and supporting documents

• Be of good character, honesty, and integrity

• Mandatory employment experience

Mississippi

Licensing Authority

Currently, a private investigator license is not required for the state of Mississippi.

The state may require a business license.

Missouri

Licensing Authority

Private Investigator licensing in Missouri is handled by the Missouri Division of Professional Registration Board of Private Investigator and Private Fire Investigator Examiners.

Contact Information

Missouri Division of Professional Registration
3605 Missouri Boulevard
P.O. Box 1335
Jefferson City, MO, 65102-1335
Telephone: 573.751.0293
TTY: 800.735.2966
Voice Relay: 800.735.2466
Email: profreg@pr.mo.gov
Website: http://pr.mo.gov/pi.asp

General Requirements

The following is general licensing information. Please visit the website listed above for specific licensing information, application forms, insurance requirements, fees, and any special licensing requirements.

Before an application for a license may be granted, the applicant shall:

• Be at least twenty-one years of age;

• Be a citizen of the United States;

• Provide proof of liability insurance with an amount to be no less than two hundred fifty thousand dollars in coverage and proof of workers' compensation insurance. The board shall have the authority to raise the requirements as deemed necessary; and

• Comply with such other qualifications as the board adopts by rules and regulations

Montana

Licensing Authority

Private Investigator licensing in the state of Montana is handled by the Montana Department of Labor and Industry, Board of Private Security. The Board of Private Security provides information on the licensing and regulation of security alarm installers, private security guards, security alarm runners, private investigators, private investigator trainees, process servers, certified firearm instructors, resident managers, and, the following related businesses; electronic security company, contract security company, proprietary security organizations and branch offices in Montana.

Contact Information

301 South Park, 4th Floor
P.O. Box 200513
Helena, MT 59620-0513
Fax: (406) 841-2305
E-mail: dlibsdpsp@mt.gov
Website: http://boards.bsd.dli.mt.gov/psp

General Requirements

The following is general licensing information. Please visit the website listed above for specific licensing information, application

forms, insurance requirements, fees, and any special licensing requirements.

- ☐ Education Requirements: High school diploma or equivalent

- ☐ Experience Requirements: three years.

Nebraska

Licensing Authority

The Nebraska Secretary of State Licensing Division handles private investigator licensing in Nebraska.

Contact Information

Nebraska Secretary of State Licensing Division
Mailing Address: P.O. Box 94608, Lincoln, NE 68509-4608
Location: State Capitol, Room 1305, 1445 K St., Lincoln, NE 68509
Phone: (402) 471-2385
Fax: (402) 471-2530
Email: licensing@nebraska.gov
Website: https://sos.nebraska.gov/licensing/private-detectives

Nevada

Licensing Authority

Private Investigator licensing in the state of Nevada is handled by the Nevada Private Investigators Licensing Board. This agency is responsible for conducting background investigations on applicants, administering compliance audits of licensees, preparing disciplinary matters for Board review, and investigating various complaints of misconduct of a licensee or unlicensed activity.

Contact Information

State of Nevada Private Investigators Licensing Board
Carson City Location:
704 W. Nye Lane, Suite 203
Carson City, Nevada 89703
(775) 687-3223
(775) 687-3226 - Fax

Las Vegas Location:
3110 S. Durango Drive, Suite 202
Las Vegas, Nevada 89117
(702) 486-3003
(702) 486-3009 - Fax
Email: pilbinfo@ag.nv.gov
Website: http://pilb.nv.gov/

State Law: https://www.leg.state.nv.us/NAC/NAC-648.html

General Requirements

The following is general licensing information. Please visit the website listed above for specific licensing information, application forms, insurance requirements, fees, and any special licensing requirements.

Applicants must:

• Be at least 21 years of age.

• Be a citizen of the United States or lawfully entitled to remain and work in the United States.

• Be of good moral character and temperate habits.

• Have not been convicted of a felony or any crime involving moral turpitude or the illegal use or possession of a dangerous weapon

• Undergo a criminal history background check through the Federal Bureau of Investigation (FBI), the Nevada Department of Public Safety (DPS), and the California Department of Justice if you have lived in or ever visited the State of California.

• Pass an exam with a score of 75% or better (only for individual applicants and qualified agent applicants)

New Hampshire

Licensing Authority

Private Investigator licensing in the state of New Hampshire is handled by the New Hampshire Department of Safety, Support Services Bureau, Permits and Licensing Unit, and Security/Detectives.

Contact Information

New Hampshire Department of Safety

Room 106 (Permits and Licensing)

33 Hazen Drive

Concord, NH

Note: Application forms must be delivered to the above address in person.

Website: https://www.nhsp.dos.nh.gov/our-services/justice-information-bureau/permits-and-licensing

General Requirements

The following is general licensing information. Please visit the website listed above for specific licensing information, application forms, insurance requirements, fees, and any special licensing requirements.

• Be a resident of the United States

• Be at least 18 years of age

• Have no record of felony convictions of any type or conviction of a misdemeanor associated with theft, honesty, fraud, use or sale of controlled substances, misdemeanor crimes of violence that in the judgment of the commissioner of safety would cast doubt on the applicant's future good behavior, domestic violence, or abuse of any type, or an active domestic violence protective order in New Hampshire or any other jurisdiction in the United States, its possessions, or territories.

• Except for employees who possess:

• A minimum of four years experience as a full-time law enforcement officer with a federal, state, county, college or university, or municipal police department, director of security or senior officer of a company or corporation, or licensed security service, full-time adjuster, risk manager, or claims investigator for an insurance carrier or adjusting company; or

• An associate of science degree or a bachelor of science degree in criminal justice or fire service from an accredited college or university, certification from the American Society for Industrial Security as a certified professional investigator, or certification from the National Association of Legal Investigators is a certified legal investigator and employment as a full-time investigator for a private investigative agency for at least two years; or

• A minimum of four years' employment as a full-time investigator for a licensed private investigator or private investigative agency; or

• A minimum of four years experience as a full-time firefighter and certification by the International Association of Arson Investigators; or

• Certification by the American Society for Industrial Security in security operations, and two years of experience providing such services; or

• Certification by the American Society for Industrial Security in executive protection, and two years of experience providing such services.

• Provide verifiable documentation of his or her qualifications at the time of application for a license

New Jersey

Licensing Authority

Private Investigator licensing in New Jersey is handled by the New Jersey State Police Private Detective Unit.

Contact Information

New Jersey State Police
Private Detective Unit
P.O. Box 7068
West Trenton, New Jersey 08628-0068
Phone: 609-341-3426 or 609-633-9352

Email: pdu@gw.njsp.org

Website: http://www.njsp.org/private-detective/private-detective-rules.shtml

General Requirements

The following is general licensing information. Please visit the website listed above for specific licensing information, application forms, insurance requirements, fees, and any special licensing requirements.

• Applicant must be 25 years of age

• Applicant must be a United States citizen

• Applicant must possess good character, competency, and integrity

• Applicant must have a minimum of five years of experience with an organized police department of the State, County, or Municipality or an investigative agency of the United States of America or possess five years of investigative experience that can be documented. Applicant must complete a comprehensive background investigation, including a criminal history fingerprint check, and credit check.

As part of the application process, a credit profile report will be reviewed for any derogatory, delinquent, and/or past-due accounts. Applicants must provide documentation addressing all derogatory accounts before licensing. Personal credit is directly related to moral character. An individual may only serve as a qualifier for one agency; however, they may hold a corporate office position for more than one company.

New Mexico

Licensing Authority

Private Investigator licensing in New Mexico is handled by the New Mexico Regulation & Licensing Department, Private Investigations Advisory Board. The Private Investigations Advisory Board licenses and oversees private investigators, private investigations managers, private investigation companies, private patrol operators, private patrol operations managers, private security guards, and polygraph examiners.

Contact Information

New Mexico Private Investigations Board
2550 Cerrillos Road, Santa Fe, NM 87505
PO Box 25101, Santa Fe, NM 87505
Phone: (505) 476-4650
Fax: (505) 476-4615
Website:
http://www.rld.state.nm.us/boards/Private_Investigations.aspx

General Requirements

The following is general licensing information. Please visit the website listed above for specific licensing information, application forms, insurance requirements, fees, and any special licensing requirements.

Applicants for licensure as a private investigator must submit the following:

• Completed application;

• Proof of age indicating the applicant is at least twenty-one (21) years of age (copy of a birth certificate, driver's license, state-issued identification card, or baptismal certificate);

• Proof of successfully passing a jurisprudence examination to be administered by the department; a surety bond in the amount of ten thousand dollars ($10,000) executed by a surety company authorized to do business in this state on a form prescribed by the department; however, private investigators who provide personal protection or bodyguard services shall maintain general liability insurance in the amount not less than one million dollars ($1,000,000) in lieu of the surety bond required by the provisions of this paragraph; proof of experience that has been acquired within the five years preceding the filing of the application with the department which shall consist of not less than 6,000 hours of actual work performed in investigation for the purpose of obtaining information with reference to a crime or wrongs done or threatened against the United States; investigation of persons; the location, disposition or recovery of lost or stolen property; the cause or responsibility for fire, losses, motor vehicle or other accidents or damage or injury to persons or property; or securing evidence to be used before a court, administrative tribunal, board or investigating committee or for a law enforcement officer; non-refundable license fee as set forth in Part 5; and Criminal history background check

• Years of qualifying experience and the precise nature of that experience shall be substantiated by written certification from employers on a form provided by the department and shall be subject to independent verification by the department as it deems warranted. In the event of the inability of applicants to supply such written certifications from employers in whole or in part, applicants may offer other written certifications from others than employers covering the same subject matter for consideration by the department. The burden of proving the necessary experience is on the applicant.

• All applicants for initial issuance, reinstatement, or renewal of a private investigator license in New Mexico shall be required to be fingerprinted to establish positive identification for a state and federal criminal history background check.

• Blank fingerprint cards shall be obtained from the department.

Fingerprints shall be taken: under the supervision of and certified by a New Mexico state police officer, a county sheriff, or a municipal chief of police; by comparable officers in the applicant's state of residence if the applicant is not a resident of New Mexico; or at the discretion of the department, by a private agency or individual qualified to take and certify fingerprints, provided the agency submits to the department written authorization or proof of training from any of the agencies

• Completed fingerprint cards shall be submitted to the department or department designee with a check, money order, or cashier's check for the prescribed fee.

• Proof of successful completion of mandatory firearms training.

New York

Licensing Authority

Private Investigator licensing in the state of New York is handled by the New York Department of State Division of Licensing Services. For additional information, see also the New York State Law governing private investigators.

Contact Information

New York Department of State Division of Licensing Services
Department of State, Albany Location:
One Commerce Plaza, 99 Washington Ave
Albany, NY 12231-0001

Department of State, New York City Location:
123 William Street, New York, NY 10038-3804
Phone: (518) 474-4429
Fax: (518) 473-6648

Website: https://dos.ny.gov/licensing-services

General Requirements

The following is general licensing information. Please visit the website listed above for specific licensing information, application forms, insurance requirements, fees, and any special licensing requirements.

- Character References

- Bonding ($10,000 surety bond)

- Proof of Training/Experience

- Personal Background Information

- Proof of liability insurance (if employing security guards)

- Applicant must be at least 25 years of age

- Electronic Fingerprints

For more detailed information, requirements, forms, and fees, please visit the New York State Business Express website at https://www.businessexpress.ny.gov/. Search for the keywords "private investigator" and review the results.

North Carolina

Licensing Authority

Private Investigator Licensing in North Carolina is handled by the Department of Public Safety Private Protective Services Board. The purpose of the Private Protective Services Board is to administer the licensing, education, and training requirements for persons, firms, associations, and corporations engaged in private protective services within North Carolina. The board is totally fee funded.

Contact Information

North Carolina Department of Public Safety
512 North Salisbury Street
Raleigh, NC 27604
919-733-2126
Website: https://www.ncdps.gov/About-DPS/Boards-Commissions/Private-Protective-Services-Board/Licensing-Process

General Requirements

The following is general licensing information. Please visit the website listed above for specific licensing information, application forms, insurance requirements, fees, and any special licensing requirements.

• All applicants must:

• Be at least 18 years of age

• Have a high school degree or equivalent

• Be a United States citizen or a resident alien

• Be of good moral character with temperate habits (no criminal record, etc.)

North Dakota

Licensing Authority

Private Investigator licensing in North Dakota is handled by the North Dakota Private Investigative & Security Board. The North Dakota Private Investigation & Security Board is a governor-appointed board that licenses and regulates the Private Investigation and Security industries.

The board establishes the qualifications and procedures for classifying, qualifying, licensing, bonding, and regulating persons providing private investigative and security services, including armed security personnel.

Contact Information

North Dakota Private Investigative & Security Board
513 Bismarck Expressway, Suite 5
Bismarck, ND 58504
Phone & Fax 701-222-3063
NDPISB@MIDCO.Net

Website: https://www.pisb.nd.gov/

General Requirements

The following is general licensing information. Please visit the website listed above for specific licensing information, application

forms, insurance requirements, fees, and any special licensing requirements.

• Be at least eighteen years of age.

• Be a high school graduate or hold the equivalent of a high school diploma.

• Have not been convicted or adjudged guilty in any jurisdiction of one of the following offenses or its equivalent in another jurisdiction, including juvenile adjudication that the individual has engaged in similar conduct: any felony; any class A or B misdemeanor involving an act of violence or intimidation; or involving controlled substances; any offense involving theft including shoplifting, or any other offense which must be reported to the North Dakota Bureau of Criminal Investigation. This subsection will not prohibit the board from issuing a license or registration to an individual if the board determines the offense does not have a direct bearing upon the individual's ability to provide private security services to the public and the individual has been sufficiently rehabilitated, or a full pardon has been granted.

• Be free of mental conditions or defects that interfere with the individual's ability to provide services professionally and competently.

• Have not committed an act that the board determines indicates bad moral character and directly affects the applicant's ability to serve the public, including but not limited to offenses other than those listed in subsection three section.

Ohio

Licensing Authority

The Ohio Department of Private Investigator and Security Guard Services handles private investigator licensing in Ohio.

Contact Information

Ohio Department of Private Investigator and Security Guard Services (PISGS)
PO Box 182001
Columbus, OH 43218-2001

Website: http://pisgs.ohio.gov/

General Requirements

The following is general licensing information. Please visit the website listed above for specific licensing information, application forms, insurance requirements, fees, and any special licensing requirements.

View the document Private Investigator Security Guard Services Laws and Rules document at http://pisgs.ohio.gov/ApplicationGuide.pdf. Also, refer to the License Reference Guide for more information about the licensing process at http://pisgs.ohio.gov/PISG_License_Reference.pdf.

Oklahoma

Licensing Authority

Private Investigator licensing in Oklahoma is handled by the Oklahoma Council on Law Enforcement Education & Training (CLEET).

Contact Information

Council on Law Enforcement Education and Training
2401 Egypt Road
ADA, Oklahoma 74820-0669
Telephone Switchboard: 405-239-5100
Local ADA Number: 580-310-0871
Main Fax: 580.310.9143 or 405.239.5180

Website: https://www.ok.gov/cleet/Licensing/Private_Investigators/

State Law: http://oklegal.onenet.net/oklegal-cgi/get_statute?98/Title.59/59-1750.1.html

General Requirements

The following is general licensing information. Please visit the website listed above for specific licensing information, application forms, insurance requirements, fees, and any special licensing requirements.

• Applicants wanting to apply for a Private Investigator license must complete the necessary training, apply for a license, and undergo a fingerprint background check. Below are the items you will need to complete a new application.

• Application with attachments completed and signature notarized

• A Certified court Judgment and Sentence or letter of no record for each arrest and/or charge, if applicable. (All questions on page 2 must be answered)

• Legible CLEET fingerprint cards with all required data

• Two current passport-size color photographs or three if applying for an armed license. Paper or plastic photos are NOT acceptable

• Local police department and sheriff department record checks

• Letter of Employment (if applicable) or bond/insurance

• Agency Application (Required if self-employed Private Investigator)

• Documented proof of experience or comparable training.

• Payment amount required. Please do not mail cash. No personal checks. Only money orders, company checks, or cashier's checks are accepted

• If not a United States Citizen, verifiable documentation of legal residence

Oregon

Licensing Authority

Private Investigator licensing in the state of Oregon is handled by the Oregon Department of Public Safety Standards and Training (DPSST).

DPSST's Private Security and Private Investigator Program provides training and licensing services to its constituents in an industry-initiated effort to enhance professionalism among member businesses and employees who provide services in Oregon. The program works together with its policy committee members and the Board on Public Safety Standards and Training to establish professional standards and provide training to assist constituents in meeting these standards and provide training to assist constituents in meeting these standards as well as to enforce licensure and certification requirements for private security professionals and private investigators.

Contact Information

Oregon Department of Public Safety Standards and Training
4190 Aumsville Hwy SE
Salem, Oregon 97317
Phone: 503-378-8531
Fax: 503-378-4600

Website: https://www.oregon.gov/dpsst/PI/Pages/Home.aspx

General Requirements

The following is general licensing information. Please visit the website listed above for specific licensing information, application forms, insurance requirements, fees, and any special licensing requirements.

• Complete a PI-1 application

• Secure a surety bond, irrevocable letter of credit, or errors & omissions insurance in the minimum amount of $5000 with your name listed as principal

• Complete one fingerprint card in a tamper-proof bag along with the fingerprint affidavit form

• Complete three professional letters of reference. References cannot be related to you by blood or marriage

• Submit proof of 1500 hours (via your resume) of professional work experience if applying for a private investigators license. No proof of experience is required if applying for a provisional investigators license. (Some educational substitution may apply)

• Complete two passport-quality photographs. (Photos should be submitted electronically at piappsubmittal@state.or.us. The digital photo must meet specific criteria; see below for an explanation. No copies or laser printer copies will be accepted)

• PI-27 (Private Investigator Professional Code of Ethics)

• Review the list of criminal disqualifiers in Oregon Administrative Rules Division 61

• Submit a one-time $70.75 application fee and the required $550 licensing fee (VISA/MC, cashier's check, money order, or business check. No personal checks or cash). Please check the website listed above for the most current fee amounts.

• Once your completed application packet is processed, you will be registered for the PI Proficiency Exam. Visit the website listed above for a calendar of class availability.

Note: If you need to obtain a temporary license in Oregon, you must obtain a private investigator bond or an irrevocable letter of credit.

* Criteria for electronic submittal: JPEG format (.jpg), minimum 640x480 resolution, cropped headshot, solid-colored background, photo date must be within the last six months, sent from an email address on file at DPSST (or) if new applicant, sent from the email address listed on the application or submitted on a CD with paper documents and driver's license quality professional photograph.

Pennsylvania

Licensing Authority

Private Investigator Licensing in Pennsylvania is handled by the Pennsylvania Courts of Common Pleas. To apply for a license, contact the clerk of the court in the county you wish to be licensed.

Contact Information

Visit the Unified Judicial System of Pennsylvania website at http://www.pacourts.us/courts/courts-of-common-pleas/prothonotaries for contact information. Contact the Clerk of Courts for your county to find out how to apply.

General Requirements

The following is general licensing information. Please visit the website listed above for specific licensing information, application forms, insurance requirements, fees, and any special licensing requirements.

To qualify for a license, an applicant must:

• Be a United States citizen

• Be at least 25 years old

• Be a member of the U.S. government investigative services OR

• Be a sheriff OR

• Be a member of the Pennsylvania State Police OR

• Have at least three years of private detective experience

• Not have been convicted of a felony

Be prepared to submit the following with your application. Note, these may vary by county:

- Fingerprint cards
- Character references
- Two photos of yourself (passport size)
- A surety bond for $10,000
- An application license fee of $200

Rhode Island

Licensing Authority

Private investigator licensing in the State of Rhode Island is handled by the city or town in which the private investigator resides.

Contact Information

Please visit the website for the city or town where you wish to be licensed. A list of links is available at http://www.ri.gov/towns/.

View details on the Rhode Island Private Investigator Act at https://law.justia.com/codes/rhode-island/2012/title-5/chapter-5-5/.

South Carolina

Licensing Authority

Private Investigator licensing in South Carolina is handled by the South Carolina State Law Enforcement Division (SLED).

Contact Information

South Carolina State Law Enforcement Division
SLED Headquarters is located at
4400 Broad River Road
Columbia, SC 29210
The public may reach SLED through telephone number (803) 737-9000 or a mailing address of
Post Office Box 21398
Columbia, SC 29221

Website: https://www.sled.sc.gov/PI_Security.html

General Requirements

The following is general licensing information. Please visit the website listed above for specific licensing information, application forms, insurance requirements, fees, and any special licensing requirements.

Applicants for private investigative business licenses or registrations will be ineligible for licensing/registration if any of the following apply:

• Not a United States citizen.

• Under 18 years of age

• Any discharge from military service that is other than honorable

• Currently holding any other position that would constitute dual-office holding and/or a conflict of interest, such as Actively commissioned law enforcement officers, Coroners, Jailers or detention officers, Probation or Parole Officers, Reserve officers, State Constables, Federal officers, investigators, or inspectors (including military police/investigators)

• Conviction of a felony or crime involving moral turpitude

• Has a criminal charge pending that, if convicted, would prohibit the individual from being licensed or registered

• Applicant fails to meet any other criteria outlined in the S.C. Private Investigative or Contract Security Agencies Act, or falsifies the application for a license and/or registration

Please visit the website for a complete list of requirements and to learn the steps involved in the application process.

South Dakota

South Dakota is one of the few states that do not require private investigators to be licensed. However, a business license must be obtained through the Department of Revenue. View the document License Requirements for Sales, Use & Contractors' Excise Tax at https://dor.sd.gov/businesses/taxes/.

This Tax Fact sheet contains the basics about sales, use, and contractors' excise tax licensing requirements and how to obtain a permit in South Dakota.

Contact Information

South Dakota Department of Revenue
445 E Capitol Avenue, Pierre, SD 57501

Website: http://dor.sd.gov/

Tennessee

Licensing Authority

Private Investigator licensing in Tennessee is handled by the Tennessee Department of Commerce & Insurance – Private Investigation and Polygraph Commission.

Contact Information

State of Tennessee
Department of Commerce and Insurance
Division of Regulatory Boards
Private Investigation and Polygraph Commission
500 James Robertson Parkway
Nashville, TN 37243-1167
Phone: 615-741-4827
Fax: 615-532-2965

Website:
https://www.tn.gov/content/tn/commerce/regboards/pi.html

General Requirements

The following is general licensing information. Please visit the website listed above for specific licensing information, application forms, insurance requirements, fees, and any special licensing requirements.

To hold a valid Tennessee Private Investigator License, the applicant/licensee must be affiliated with a licensed Tennessee Private Investigators Company. Each applicant for a private investigator license must:

(1) Be at least twenty-one (21) years of age;

(2) Be a citizen of the United States or a resident alien;

(3) Not have been declared by any court of competent jurisdiction incompetent because of a mental defect or disease unless a court of competent jurisdiction has since declared the applicant competent;

(4) Not be suffering from habitual drunkenness or narcotics addiction or dependence;

(5) Be of good moral character; and

(6) Pass an examination designed to measure knowledge and competence in the investigations field. Examination information can be found here.

(7) Be affiliated with a licensed PI Company.

Texas

Licensing Authority

Private Investigator licensing in Texas is handled by the Texas Department of Public Safety/Private Security Bureau. The bureau regulates the private security and private investigation industry under the authority of the Texas Occupations Code, Chapter 1702, and the Private Security Board's Administrative Rules.

Contact Information

Please visit the Texas Department of Public Safety/Private Security Bureau website at http://www.dps.texas.gov/rsd/psb/. Application forms can be submitted online, and questions can be submitted via an online form.

Street Address:
Texas Department of Public Safety
5805 North Lamar Blvd.
Austin, Texas 78752-4431

Mailing Address:
Texas Department of Public Safety
P O Box 4087
Austin, Texas 78773-0001

General Requirements

The following is general licensing information. Please visit the website listed above for specific licensing information, application forms, insurance requirements, fees, and any special licensing requirements.

You may apply for a private investigator license if:

• You are at least 18 years old

• You have never been convicted of a felony in any jurisdiction

• You have not been convicted in the past five years of a Class B misdemeanor in any jurisdiction

• You are not currently charged with or under indictment for a Class A misdemeanor or felony

• You are not currently charged with a Class B misdemeanor

• You have never been found incompetent due to mental defect or disease by a court

• You are not required to register in Texas or any other jurisdiction as a sex offender

• You have never been dishonorably discharged from U.S. military service

Utah

Licensing Authority

Private Investigator licensing in Utah is handled by the Utah Department of Public Safety, Bureau of Criminal Identification. Visit the website to obtain the most updated and specific information on the requirements, download application forms, and understand the education and exam requirements to become a private investigator in Utah.

Contact Information

Bureau of Criminal Identification
3888 West 5400 South
Taylorsville, UT 84129
801-965-4445

Website: https://bci.utah.gov/private-investigator-licensing/

General Requirements

The following is general licensing information. Please visit the website listed above for specific licensing information, application forms, insurance requirements, fees, and any special licensing requirements.

You may apply for a private investigator license if you are:

• At least 21 years of age

- A legal resident of Utah

- Of a good moral character

Vermont

Licensing Authority

Private Investigator licensing in Vermont is handled by the Vermont Secretary of State Board of Private Investigative and Security Services.

The five-member board was created by the legislature whose members are appointed by the governor to administer the laws for this profession in the state of Vermont. The board's mission is public protection. The board does this by ensuring that applicants are qualified for licensure; setting standards for the profession by proposing statutes and adopting administrative rules; and, with the assistance of Office of Professional Regulation staff, investigating complaints of unprofessional conduct, taking disciplinary action against licensees when necessary to protect the public.

Contact Information

Office of Professional Regulation
89 Main Street, 3rd Floor
Montpelier VT 05620-3402

Website: https://sos.vermont.gov/private-investigative-security-services/

General Requirements

The following is general licensing information. Please visit the website listed above for specific licensing information, application forms, insurance requirements, fees, and any special licensing requirements.

You may apply for a private investigator license if:

• You are at least 18 years old

• You have two years of investigative experience

• You are a citizen of the United States or a legal resident

• You have completed the required training

Virginia

Licensing Authority

Private Investigator licensing in Virginia is handled by the Virginia Department of Criminal Justice Services, Division of Licensure and Regulatory Affairs.

The Virginia Department of Criminal Justice Services, Private Security Services reviews and processes all applications for registration, certification, and licensure for individuals, businesses, and training schools that provide private security services. The Virginia Private Security Services is also responsible for providing technical assistance and has statutory authority to proceed with enforcement action against private investigators in an effort to protect the public from unlicensed and unethical business practices.

Contact Information

Please visit the Virginia Department of Criminal Justice Services, Division of Licensure and Regulatory Affairs website at https://www.dcjs.virginia.gov/licensure-and-regulatory-affairs/private-investigator.

General Requirements

The following is general licensing information. Please visit the website listed above for specific licensing information, application

forms, insurance requirements, fees, and any special licensing requirements.

• Be a minimum of 18 years of age

• Successful completion of all initial training requirements for each registration category, including firearms endorsement if applicable

• Be a United States citizen or legal resident alien of the United States

Reciprocity Agreements

Virginia has reciprocity agreements with North Carolina, Georgia, Tennessee, Oklahoma, Louisiana, and Florida.

Washington

Licensing Authority

Private Investigator licensing in Washington is handled by the Washington Department of Licensing, Business & Professional Licensing.

Contact Information

Private investigator agencies
Phone: 800.451.7985
Fax: 360.705.6699
Email: BLS@dor.wa.gov

Mailing address:

State of Washington

Business Licensing Service

PO Box 9034, Olympia, WA 98507-9034

Physical location:

Business Licensing Service

6500 Linderson Way SW, Tumwater, WA 98501

Armed private investigators, unarmed private investigators, and certified trainers

Phone: 360.664.6611

Fax: 360.570.7888

Email: security@dol.wa.gov

Mail forms with payments to:

Private Investigator Program

Department of Licensing

PO Box 35001, Seattle, WA 98124-3401

Mail correspondence with no payments to:

Private Investigators

Department of Licensing

PO Box 9649, Olympia, WA 98507-9649

Physical location

Department of Licensing

405 Black Lake Blvd SW, Olympia, WA 98502

Website: http://www.dol.wa.gov/business/pi/

General Requirements

The department has different licensing requirements for a Private Investigator Agency, and Armed Private Investigator, and an Unarmed Private Investigator. Since those requirements may change without notice, the most up-to-date information will be on the department's website at the address above. On the website, you'll find:

- How to renew your private detective license
- Application forms and fees required
- State exam study resources
- Training requirements and resources
- How to look up a professional license
- How to file a complaint on a private detective

Training

Washington has a list of specific exam study resources on its licensing website. Exam study topics include:

- Washington state law as it applies to private investigator licensing and regulation
- Federal laws

- Court systems
- State courts
- Legal procedures and definitions
- Resources for public information

Washington D.C.

Licensing Authority

Private Investigator licensing in Washington D.C. is handled by the Washington D.C. Department of Consumer and Regulatory Affairs, Occupational and Professional License Administration, and Board of Security.

Contact Information

1100 4th Street, SW, Washington, DC 20024

Phone: (202) 442-4400

Fax: (202) 442-9445

TTY: (202) 123-4567

Email: dcra@dc.gov

Website: https://dcra.dc.gov/

General Requirements

The following is general licensing information. Please visit the website listed above for specific licensing information, application forms, insurance requirements, fees, and any special licensing requirements.

To qualify for a license in Washington D.C.:

• Applicants must be at least 18.

• Any individual applying for a Private Detective License must not have any felony conviction(s) within the last two years and no Misdemeanor conviction(s) within the last year. You must submit any information relative to the charge if you have a prior criminal history. (i.e., court dispositions, receipt of payment for fines, letter of successful completion of probation, etc.)

• A criminal history inquiry for each applicant will be verified through an FBI fingerprint analysis. Background checks require approximately ninety (90) days to complete.

• Applicants must submit a notarized Arrest Affidavit and Employment & Residence Form indicating the applicant's past employment, residence(s), and arrest history.

• Must submit two (2) passport-type photos of the applicant's face, measuring approximately 2" x 2" with the applicant's name printed on the back. Please note that home snapshots and home computer photographs are not acceptable.

• Must submit a copy of an Official Government Issued Photo ID such as a driver's license.

• Must submit a completed application, including required supporting documents and total fees. You will not be invoiced later for the license fee.

• Must submit a notarized Authorization to Release Information Form.

• Fingerprinting required for certification will be processed at the Security Officers' Management Branch (SOMB). Contact SOMB for hours of operation at 202-671-0500. Fingerprinting requires a company check or money order for thirty-five dollars ($35.00) made payable to the D.C. Treasurer. Applicants from another city or state may mail completed fingerprint cards (ink prints) to the SOMB from their local jurisdiction. In such a case, two fingerprint cards are required per applicant for licensure. The mailing address is Metropolitan Police Department, Security Officers Management Branch, 2000 14th Street, N.W., Room #302, Washington, DC 20009

IMPORTANT NOTE: The following documents must be presented at the time of fingerprinting: 1) Notarized Authorization to Release Information Form, 2) Notarized Arrest Affidavit and Resident & Employment Log

Applicant must submit a copy of the birth certificate as required by the state vital statistics agency (hospital birth certificate not valid) and legal documentation of name change (marriage certificate, divorce decree, adoption papers, etc.) if applicable. A copy of a valid U.S. passport may be submitted in place of the birth certificate. Original birth certificates and name change documents submitted will not be returned.

If the applicant is not a U.S. Citizen, proof of immigration status must be submitted, for example, a Resident Alien Card (Green

Card), Employment Authorization, Certificate of Naturalization, or I-94 Departure Record.

A person who submits an application for licensing as a PD must also submit a copy of a Certificate of Release from Active Duty (DD-214); if an applicant has prior military service. Please submit copy #4, which shows the type of separation from the service.

Private Investigators (Detectives) are NOT permitted to carry weapons in the District of Columbia and are not required to wear uniforms. The following services are NOT authorized in the District of Columbia: VIP Protection, Executive Protection, and/or Bodyguard Services

A $30.00 service fee is required for lost, stolen, replacement, and transferring of all Security Officers and Special Police Officer Licenses. A police report must be filed in the jurisdiction of the occurrence of all licenses stolen and/or lost. The report numbers must be submitted to SOMB along with the reporting officer's name and badge number. A police report number must be submitted to Pearson VUE to receive a replacement.

Compared to other states, Washington, D.C. has more detailed requirements for applicants. I recommend visiting the Department of Consumer and Regulatory Affairs website for the most up-to-date information, fees, and contact information.

West Virginia

Licensing Authority

If you want to become a private investigator in West Virginia, licensing in the state is handled by the West Virginia Secretary of State – Private Investigator and Security Guard Licensing.

Contact Information

Secretary of State
Bldg. 1, Suite 157-K
1900 Kanawha Blvd. East
Charleston, WV 25305-0770

Phone Numbers:
Main (304) 558-6000
Business and Licensing (304) 558-8000
Toll-Free (866) 767-8683
Investigation Hotline (877) 372-8398
Fax Number: (304) 558-0900

Website: https://sos.wv.gov/business/Pages/PISGLicInfo.aspx

General Requirements

The following is general licensing information. Please visit the website listed above for specific licensing information, application

forms, insurance requirements, fees, and any special licensing requirements.

You may apply for a private investigator license if you:

• Are at least 18 years old or older

• Are a citizen of the United States or an alien legally residing in the United States

• Of a good moral character

• Have not had a previous private investigator or security guard license revoked or denied in West Virginia or any other state

• Have not been declared incompetent by a court because of a mental defect or illness

• Do not suffer from narcotics addiction or dependence or habitual drunkenness

• Have not been convicted of a felony in this state or any other state or territory

• Have not been convicted of any of these crimes: Illegally using, carrying or possessing a pistol or other dangerous weapon; Making or possessing burglar's instruments; Buying or receiving stolen property; Entering a building unlawfully; Aiding an inmate's escape from prison; Possessing or distributing illicit drugs, or any misdemeanor involving moral turpitude or for which dishonesty of character is a necessary element

• Have never engaged in the private investigation or security guard business without a license;

• Have never transferred my license to an unlicensed person or subcontracted with an unlicensed person or firm to conduct investigations or security guard business;

• Have never employed anyone to conduct investigations or security guard business that was in violation of any of the prohibitions or requirements of the law;

• Have never falsely represented that I am or any other person is licensed as an investigator or guard;

• Have never made any false report with respect to any matter relating to my employment;

• Have never divulged any information obtained from or for a client without express permission;

• Have never knowingly accepted employment to obtain information intended for illegal purposes; or

• Have never authorized another person to violate the law or rules.

Wisconsin

Licensing Authority

Private Investigator licensing in Wisconsin is handled by the Wisconsin Department of Safety and Professional Services.

Contact Information

Wisconsin Department of Safety and Professional Services

Division of Professional Credential Processing

1400 East Washington Avenue

PO Box 8935

Madison, WI 53708-8935

Phone: 608-266-2112

Email: dsps@wisconsin.gov

Website: https://dsps.wi.gov/pages/Home.aspx

General Requirements

The following is general licensing information. Please visit the website listed above for specific licensing information, application forms, insurance requirements, fees, and any special licensing requirements.

Applicants must take and pass an examination covering Wisconsin statutes and administrative code, and investigative practices relevant to functioning as a private detective.

The Department of Safety & Professional Services administers the exam. The exam will be available from home, work, or public computer. To register for the exam, download, complete, and submit the Application for Private Detective License (form #469).

After receipt and processing of a complete application, directions for accessing the exam will be e-mailed to you. The passing score for this exam is 84%.

If you fail the exam, you must retake the exam by downloading the retake application HERE and submitting it along with a $75.00 retake fee to the Department. You will then be assigned another test. Please visit the website listed above for current fee notices.

The exam content is drawn from applicable state statutes and administrative code chapters specific to the profession. The purpose of the exam is to familiarize you with locating the statutes and administrative code that regulate the practice of the profession.

Exam results are good for one year. You must be licensed within a year from the date you passed the exam, or you will have to retake and pass the exam before you can be licensed. You may take the exam as many times as you want.

Wyoming

Currently, Wyoming does not have state-level requirements for private investigators to be licensed. However, some individual state municipalities may regulate private investigators and security alarm companies via city ordinances. You should check with the specific municipalities where you plan to conduct business. For example, Cheyenne requires private investigators to have a business license.

Private investigators in the state are subject to the same laws and regulations as law enforcement. Also, if you operate a security firm, you may need to register with the Secretary of State.

Also, if your company conducts business in Wyoming, contact the Wyoming Department of Revenue if you are subject to the state revenue laws.

Visit the Wyoming Division of Criminal Investigation (DCI) at http://wyomingdci.wyo.gov/ for more information.

Chapter 7: Getting Your Business Up and Running

Now that you're officially licensed in the state to conduct private investigations, the next step is to start and run your own private investigation business. Learn about business licensing and insurance coverage requirements. In addition, learn about the equipment and supplies you'll need, how to establish an online presence, website, social media, email, and more.

Determine if you need a Business License

Many states require a business license in addition to a private investigator's license. Check with the state licensing authority to learn about the specific requirements for your state.

Get Insurance: Protect Your Private Investigation Business

Insurance requirements for private investigators will vary from state to state and will also vary based on the type of work being performed. In most cases, private investigators will need the same type of coverage as any business, but there are some unique situations to consider. Due to the nature of private investigation work, you could find yourself liable in a number of situations, such as bodily injury, financial losses, negligence, auto accidents, worker's compensation, and more.

The types of insurance a private investigator may need:

General Liability Insurance - General liability insurance provides coverage for bodily injury or property damage to another person.

Commercial Automobile Liability Insurance - If you're doing surveillance work or searching for missing persons, you'll likely spend a lot of time on the road. Auto insurance will provide coverage for auto accidents.

Workers Compensation - If you have employees, you may be required to carry this type of insurance to cover accidents that your employees have while doing business.

Property Insurance - This type of insurance will only be necessary to protect the building you operate if you own it.

There are other specialized types of insurance that may be necessary depending on the type of work being performed. Discuss the details with your agent and lawyer, and contact multiple insurance companies to get price quotes before deciding.

Decide Whether You Need Office Space

A very important decision you'll need to make is whether to set up a physical office space. An office will provide you with a place to conduct your private investigation business, meet with clients, interview witnesses, and store materials, equipment, and supplies. In addition to its functional benefits, physical office space may help promote your business, especially if it is located in a high-traffic area. Street and window signage will serve as helpful marketing and advertising tools to let people know about your business and your services. The downside of having a physical office space is, of course, the cost. The potential expenses associated with maintaining an office include rent, utilities, equipment, supplies, parking, and other expenses.

On the other hand, a private investigation business can be run without a physical office. A private investigator can run the business out of a personal residence. Meetings with clients and witnesses can be conducted in convenient public places such as restaurants and coffee houses. The money saved from not paying for an office can be redirected to marketing and advertising efforts or toward additional profit for your business.

Buy Equipment and Supplies

Whether you decide to run your business in a physical office space or out of your home, you'll need to purchase equipment used to run your private investigation business. The type of equipment and supplies you need will depend largely on the services you plan to provide. Following are some ideas for the basic items you'll need to get started:

Computer or laptop - If you plan to offer data retrieval services, background checks, missing person locates, or similar services, you'll need a computer with an internet connection. In addition, you'll need a computer to prepare reports for clients, develop marketing and advertising materials, manage your website and social media accounts, and send/receive emails.

Computer accessories and peripherals - In addition to a computer/laptop, you may need peripheral devices such as a printer, scanner, and fax machine. Consider how you'll be communicating with clients before investing in this equipment.

Camera - If you plan to offer surveillance services, you'll need to invest in a high-quality digital quality camera. When you evaluate various camera models, consider how and where the camera will be used. You'll need a camera that is portable, durable, take high-quality photos, and has key features like optical zoom. And don't forget the extras such as a durable camera case, spare batteries, memory cards, and special filters and lenses.

Office supplies - You will need office materials such as pens and pencils, notepads (for taking notes), copier/printer paper, etc. I recommend buying these as you need them. Don't tie up your cash flow in office supply inventory.

Smartphone - Private investigators spend much time communicating, especially on the phone. Investigators spend time on the phone with clients, law enforcement, attorneys, information providers, courthouses, and others. A high-quality, durable smartphone is a necessity for private investigative work. In addition to making calls, investigators use smartphones to run a variety of apps to perform searches, navigate around town, send and receive email, etc. Also, your smartphone camera will serve as an important backup if you don't have your digital camera with you.

Optional

Badge - In most states, private investigators are required to carry a copy of their private investigator license, but they are not required to carry a badge. However, some private investigators choose to carry a badge as a form of proof and prestige. However, it is important to note that carrying a badge carries no official "weight" and does not mean you have any special capabilities or authority.

Sign up with Database Information Providers

If you plan to offer data retrieval services, such as background checks, missing person searches, social media investigations, and employment history reports, you'll need access to a database information service, such as:

• Accurint, by LexisNexis, website http://www.accurint.com/

• Clear for Investigations, by Thomson Reuters, website http://legalsolutions.thomsonreuters.com/law-products/solutions/clear-investigation-software

• Intellicorp, website https://www.intellicorp.net/marketing

• IRB Search, website http://www.irbsearch.com/

- , by TransUnion, website https://www.tlo.com/investigators

Investigate these companies to determine the solutions you'll need for your particular menu of services. Contact the service providers that best meet your needs and schedule a demo.

Establish an Online Presence

Establishing an online presence for your business is one of the most important steps in setting up your private investigation business. An online presence includes your business website, email account, social media accounts, and directory listings. These will represent your business twenty-four hours a day, seven days a week, and 365 days a year, so it is important to get them right.

Create a Website

There are many options to set up a website. The most economical route is to create your own using a free service such as Blogger, Wix.com, or Weebly.com. These sites offer easy-to-follow wizards for setting up a website with pre-built templates and themes. These sites also provide web hosting services, so you don't have to deal with that separately. Additional costs are necessary when you decide to upgrade or install add-ons. I recommend using these sites if you're new to the web.

If you are comfortable with basic website design and development, you can save money by doing everything yourself. With this approach, you'll need to:

- Register a domain name through a registrar

- Establish an account with a web hosting company

- Install a content management package, such as WordPress, Joomla, Drupal, etc.

- Create and configure email accounts

- Build website content; add photos, links to other sites, etc.

If you have the budget, hire a web development company to create a website to your specifications

Setup Email

I recommend that you set up a website first. Many web hosting providers include a certain number of email accounts with any hosting package. The primary benefit of using the email account associated with your website hosting is the domain name will be the same. For example, if your domain name is www.floridabestinvestigator.com, then your email account would use the same domain name, such as gumshoe@floridasbestinvestigator.com. This has two benefits. First, every email you send will help promote your website. Second, it is far more professional. It suggests that you are running a serious business, rather than running a "fly by night" operation with a cheap email service provider.

Setup Social Media Accounts

As a private investigator, social media allows you to promote yourself, your ideas, your business, and the services you provide to a worldwide audience. There are hundreds of social media networks, but I recommend focusing your efforts on just a few: Facebook, Twitter, LinkedIn, Instagram, Pinterest, and Google Business. Create an account in your company's name on Facebook, Twitter, and Google Plus.

For each of these networks, do the following:

• First, create an account in your company name

• Fill out the entire profile to describe your company and services

• Add photos to enhance the look and feel of your profile

• Search the network for private investigators and those in related industries, such as process servers, attorneys, bodyguards, security guards, etc.

• Send requests to connect to start building your network

• Post regularly on each network. Posts can include such things as work you recently completed, website updates, interesting investigation news or articles, etc.

Directory Listings

There are several good private investigator directories available online at a reasonable cost. These directories can help potential clients learn about your services and can be a solid source of business. I recommend signing up with at least one directory for at least one year. During that time, evaluate the website traffic, emails, and overall private investigation business you receive. Then, renew your listing only if the business you receive exceeds the cost of the directory.

Join an industry association

I highly recommend joining an industry association to help promote your private investigation business. Private investigation industry associations are organizations that promote the private investigation profession. They can be focused on the state and/or the national level. In addition, there are many that focus on specific aspects of the industry, such as forensics, etc.

Chapter 8: State Private Investigator Associations

Professional private investigator associations are a great resource for those who are interested in pursuing an investigative career and for those who are already working in the business. Industry associations provide access to invaluable resources such as training and continuing education opportunities, networking events and conferences, legislative lobbying power, and can be a source of referral business through information and case sharing.

The primary mission of a typical association is to promote a standard of excellence among individual investigators, enhance public confidence in the profession, provide training and development opportunities and represent the industry in public and political forums.

I recommend that you join at least one association and become an active member. Being active means that you should attend and participate in scheduled meetings, attend seminars and training offered by the association, run for a board position, participate in volunteer activities, etc.

List of State Private Investigator Associations

Following is a state-by-state list of the major private investigator associations. Please note that some states do not have an organized association.

Alabama

Alabama Private Investigators Association (APIA) – The APIA is dedicated to bringing one voice to all investigators in the State of Alabama and common standards and training. The APIA's website has information on members, the association's by-laws, committees, meetings, and contact information. The APIA lobbied heavily to encourage the state to begin regulating private investigators.

Alaska

Alaska Investigators Association – When we last checked, the Alaska Association's website was unavailable.

Arizona

Arizona Association of Licensed Private Investigators (AALPI) – The AALPI association website provides membership information, links to investigative information, conferences, and recent news. Visit the AALPI website at http://www.aalpi.com/.

Arkansas

Arkansas Association of Professional Private Investigators (AAPPI)

Private Investigator's Association of Arkansas (PIAA)

California

California Association of Licensed Investigators (CALI) – CALI is the largest private investigator association in the world. Join and take advantage of their broad membership base to network and learn from others. Visit the CALI website at http://www.cali-pi.org/.

Certified Investigative Professionals (CIPI) – CIPI is a membership organization consisting of investigative professionals and affiliates, whose mission is to promote a standard of excellence among individual investigators, enhance public confidence in the profession, and represent the industry in business, education, and political forums.

California Associate Photocopiers and Process Servers (CCAPPS)

California Association of Polygraph Examiners – Visit their website at http://www.californiapolygraph.com/.

Colorado

Colorado Society of Private Investigators – This association was formed by a group of prominent Denver private eyes with the goal of elevating the private investigation profession. Visit the website to get information on membership, association bylaws, meetings, schedules, private eye resources, and more. Visit their website at http://www.coloradoprivateinvestigators.org/.

Professional Private Investigators Association of Colorado (PPIAC) – The PPIAC is dedicated to developing and maintaining professionalism for private investigators in Colorado. The private detective association provides training opportunities and resources for private investigators statewide. The PPIAC also serves as a voice for investigators in the state legislature. Visit their website at http://ppiac.org/.

Connecticut

The Connecticut Association Of Licensed Private Investigators – The Association is a respected organization consisting of licensed investigative professionals whose mission is to assure that members of the profession provide the highest quality of service to individual, corporate, and government clients.

Delaware

Delaware Association of Detective Agencies (DADA) – Contact steve.engebretsen@state.de.us for more information.

Florida

Florida Association of Licensed Investigators (FALI) – The FALI is the largest private investigation association in the State of Florida. The FALI website provides up-to-date information and news on the investigation industry, as well as an extensive amount of resources for existing and aspiring private eyes. Visit the FALI website at https://www.fali.org/.

Florida Association of Private Investigators (FAPI) – FAPI is a professional organization created to provide a voice for licensed private investigators and related professionals within the State of Florida and throughout the United States. FAPI offers its members extensive networking opportunities with other experienced investigators nationwide, and a place to share referrals, questions, sources of information, and more in a friendly, non-competitive, yet professional atmosphere through our members-only discussion group and forums. Visit the FAPI website at http://www.myfapi.org/.

Georgia

Georgia Association of Professional Private Investigators – An association created to help educate members, enforce the P.I. code of ethics, and to establish trust among members and other investigative agencies in Georgia and the United States of America. GAPPI also educates members regarding legislative issues that directly affect the investigative industry. Visit their website at http://www.gappi.org.

Idaho

Private Investigators Association of Idaho (PIAI) – The PIAI is a professional organization created to provide a voice for private detectives and related professionals within the State of Idaho and throughout the United States. The Association offers its members extensive professional networking opportunities with other experienced investigators nationwide, and a place to share referrals, questions, sources of information, and more in a friendly, non-competitive, yet professional atmosphere throughout the state. Visit the PIAI website at http://www.piai.us/.

Illinois

Associated Detectives & Security Agencies of Illinois (ADSAI) – The ADSAI, formerly known as ADI is a state-chartered, not-for-profit organization organized for the betterment of the Detective and Security Professions. Visit the ADSAI website at http://www.adsai.org/.

Indiana

Indiana Association of Professional Investigators (IAPI) – A professional organization of detectives. Visit the IAPI website at https://iapi.net/.

Iowa

Iowa Association of Private Investigators (IAPI) – The IAPI is a valuable asset for Iowa investigators and the general public. Association members have access to multiple sources of professional benefits including continuing education and training, publications, legislative monitoring, and networking among members. The public can use the IAPI website to locate an Iowa investigator and to learn about the private investigation business. Visit their website at http://iowa-investigators.com/.

Kansas

Kansas Association of Private Investigators (KAPI) – The KAPI is a non-profit corporation that was formed to establish and perpetuate high ethical and professional standards and excellence of professional service in the private investigative industry in accordance with the association's Code of Ethics.

Kansas Association of Licensed Investigators (KALI) – The KALI is a comprehensive organization of detectives and investigative agencies serving the citizens and other organizations for all of their investigative needs. Visit the KALI website at https://www.k-a-l-i.org/.

Kentucky

Kentucky Professional Investigators Association (KPIA) – Kentucky's officially recognized organization of professional investigators. The KPIA association and website provide a variety of helpful resources for existing and aspiring private eyes.

Louisiana

Louisiana Private Investigators Association – The LPIA was founded to promote and maintain the highest ethical practices in the profession of private investigators. The LPIA website provides information for existing and aspiring private detectives, member benefits, history, events, and links of interest. The LPIA is a non-profit professional trade organization and not a licensing authority.

Maine

Maine Licensed Private Investigators Association (MLA) – The Maine Licensed Private Investigators Association is Maine's premier association of Investigators representing licensed, bonded, ethical and professional investigators throughout Maine and New England. The MLPIA actively promotes ethical, professional conduct and business operation for the profession in the press, legislature, and among peers in Maine and New England. Visit the MLPIA website at https://mlpia.org/.

Maryland

Professional Investigators Alliance of Maryland (PIAM) – professionals with common interests, goals, and needs formed PIAM. The purpose of the Alliance included but was not limited to advancing the profession of certified investigators, representing the profession before the legislature, working to eliminate unreliable, incompetent, and unlicensed individuals, promoting and maintaining the highest ethical standards, and offering resources for continuing education. P.I.A.M represents private eye interests in the investigative industry in the State of Maryland.

Maryland Investigators and Security Association (MISA) – MISA is an association of investigative and security professionals in Maryland.

Massachusetts

Licensed Private Detectives Association of Massachusetts (LPDAM) – Provides information, resources, and networking opportunities for licensed and aspiring investigators in the state. Visit the LPDAM website at https://www.lpdam.org/.

Michigan

Michigan Council of Professional Investigators (MCPI) – Visit the MCPI website at http://www.mcpihome.com/.

Minnesota

Minnesota Association of Private Investigators and Protective Agents (MAPI) – The MAPI is a non-profit corporation organized under and according to the provisions found in the Minnesota State Nonprofit Corporation Act. MAPI was initially organized and founded by private investigators interested in building career awareness through shared resources and educational opportunities. MAPI was exclusively organized as a fraternal association for educational, political, legal, and social purposes. The corporation works solely for the benefit of its members and respective industries. Visit the MCPI website at https://www.mapi.org/.

Mississippi

Mississippi Professional Investigators Association (MPIA) – The MPIA is comprised of professional private investigators in Mississippi and is a not-for-profit professional organization. The goal of the association is to advance the investigator and security profession through education and legislation. Visit the MPIA website at http://www.mpia.org/.

Missouri

Missouri State Investigators Associations (MSIA) – The MSIA is an association under the authority of the laws of the state of Missouri and is registered with the Missouri Secretary of State. The purposes of the Missouri State Investigators Association are to promote the free exchange of inter-agency information necessary to effectively carry out the work of association members; provide continuing educational efforts, get members engaged in investigative work, and; enhance the status of criminal, civil, and regulatory investigative work as a profession. Visit the website at http://www.mosia.com/.

Montana

Montana Associations of Private Investigators and Security Officers (MAPISO) – The MAPISO is an organization of professional Private Investigators and Security Operators who are properly insured and who have passed the stringent licensing requirements as established by the State of Montana Department of Labor.

Nebraska

Nebraska Association of Licensed Private Investigators (NALPI) – The NALPI is an association of a diverse group of licensed private investigators and related professionals, from across the entire state of Nebraska. NALPI is a fraternal association to promote and maintains the highest educational standards and ethical practices in the fields of investigation and related practices. Visit their website at http://www.nalpi.org/.

New Hampshire

New Hampshire League of Investigators – The League is the only Association in New Hampshire for Professional Investigators. The League provides training, networking, and representation not only before the Legislature but on the Governor's Advisory Board on Private Investigation and

Security Services. We are the voice of the Professional NH Private Investigator. Visit the NHLI website at http://www.nhli.net/.

New Jersey

New Jersey Licensed Private Investigators Association – Leverage the state's professional organization to network with other agencies, refer business, generate new ideas, and connect with specialists. Visit the NJPIA website at http://www.njlpia.org.

New York

Associated Licensed Detectives of New York State (ALDONYS) – ALDONYS is the largest New York State organization solely representing the interests of licensed private investigators and watch, guard, and patrol agencies. Visit the ALDONYS website at http://www.aldonys.org/.

North Dakota

At the time I wrote this ebook, I could not find any information about private detective associations in North Dakota.

Ohio

Ohio Association of Security & Investigative Services (OASIS) – The Ohio Association of Private Detective Agencies, Inc. is a not-for-profit corporation that serves

Private Security and Investigation Professionals with news, information, and members contact information. Visit the OASIS website at http://www.ohoasis.com/.

Ohio Investigators Association (OIA) – The OIA is a professional organization of state investigators and compliance and law enforcement personnel dedicated to encouraging professionalism and cooperation between members and their agencies. Visit the OIA website at http://www.oia.homestead.com/oia.html.

Oklahoma

Oklahoma State Private Investigator Association (OPIA) - OPIA was formed to help increase public and industry awareness, promote the interests, and raise the professional standards of the Private Investigation Profession in Oklahoma. This professional association is dedicated to being an educational resource, social networking, and political organization for the enhancement of its members. Since its inception, the organization has been instrumental in helping to protect the detective profession from unfair legislation and has sponsored legislation that is healthy for the investigative industry. Visit the OPIA website at http://www.opia.website/.

Oregon

Oregon State Private Investigator Association (OALI) – OALI is the state of Oregon's oldest and largest investigator association with paid membership. The OALI membership consists of investigative professionals and associates whose mission is to promote excellence among individual investigators, enhance public confidence in the profession, provide training, and represent the industry in public and political forums. Visit the OALI website at https://www.oali.org/.

Rhode Island

Licensed Private Detectives Association of Rhode Island (LPDARI) - professional investigators formed LPDARI to provide networking and education opportunities for private detectives. The association had grown into an informational association that works hard to influence legislation that benefits the private detective profession in the state. Visit the LPDARI website at https://www.lpdari.org/.

South Carolina

South Carolina Association of Legal Investigators (SCALI) – SCALI is a non-profit professional association for licensed private detectives and professional investigators employed by law firms and public defenders. Students and individuals who study or work within the criminal justice system may join the association as associate members. Visit the SCALI website at http://www.scalinv.com/.

Tennessee

Tennessee Professional Investigators Associations (TPIA) – TPIA was created to represent the interests of private eyes in the state legislature and provides training and education resources for its members. Visit the TPIA website at https://www.tpia.com/.

Tennessee Association of Licensed Private Investigators (TALPI) – TALPI is a self-regulating group of independent, professional investigators who work to increase awareness and educate the public about investigative services in Tennessee. TALPI offers information about groundbreaking methods and technology through continuing education courses and monthly meetings. Visit the TALPI website at https://www.talpi.org/.

Texas

Texas Association of Licensed Investigators (TALI) - An organization that promotes and encourages professionalism among licensed private investigators through information, education, training, legislative action, membership support, and networking. TALI provides helpful information on private eye training and continuing education, meeting and networking opportunities, and information resources for its members. Visit the TALI website at http://www.tali.org/.

Utah

Private Investigators Association of Utah (PIAU) - The PIAU provides helpful information for existing and aspiring private detectives. Visit the website to get the latest information and news about what is happening in the private detective industry in the state of Utah. Visit the PIAU website at https://piau.com/.

Vermont

At the time of this writing, I couldn't find any information on Vermont associations.

Virginia

Private Investigators Association of Virginia (PIAVA) – PIAVA is a professional association of detectives registered with the Department of Criminal Justice Services (DCJS) in Virginia. Membership in the Association is also available to Private eyes licensed in states other than Virginia, and individuals who work in areas related to the private security industry. PIAVA is a network of private investigative personnel and security industry professionals who share information, resources, and business opportunities. Visit the PIAVA website at https://www.piava.org/.

Other Industry Associations

In addition to state private investigator associations, private investigators may find it helpful to join specialized industry associations to the focus of their work or their particular interests. Following is a list of industry associations related to private investigations:

American Polygraph Association – The American Polygraph Association (APA) is dedicated to providing a valid and reliable means to verify the truth and establish the highest standards of moral, ethical, and professional conduct in the polygraph field. Visit the website at http://www.polygraph.org/.

American Society for Industrial Security (ASIS) – ASIS International is the preeminent organization for security professionals. ASIS is dedicated to increasing the effectiveness and productivity of security professionals by developing educational programs and materials that address broad security interests, such as the ASIS Annual Seminar and Exhibits, as well as specific security topics. Visit the website at https://www.asisonline.org/Pages/default.aspx.

The Association of Certified Fraud Examiners (ACFE) – The ACFE is the world's largest anti-fraud organization and premier anti-fraud training and education provider.

Association of Christian Investigators – The Association of Christian Investigators (ACI) is designed to provide an environment where an investigator can create meaningful and long-term relationships with other investigators who share common interests outside of professional bonds. Visit the website at http://www.a-c-i.org/.

National Association of Consumer Reporting Agencies (NCRA) – The NCRA is a national trade organization of consumer reporting agencies and associated professionals that provide products and services to hundreds of thousands of credit grantors, employers, landlords, and all types of general businesses. Visit the website at http://www.ncrainc.org/.

Association of Forensic Document Examiners, AFDE – The Association of Forensic Document Examiners was formed as a professional organization for forensic document examiners. Our original goals were to provide quality continuing education, promote research within the field, establish a board certification program, and publish a journal devoted exclusively to document examination. Visit the website at http://www.afde.org/.

Certified Investigative Professionals (CIPI) – CIPI is a membership organization consisting of investigative professionals and affiliates whose mission is to promote a standard of excellence among individual investigators, enhance public confidence in the profession, and represent the industry in business, education, and political forums.

High Technology Crime Investigation Association (HTCIA) – The HTCIA is designed to encourage, promote, aid, and affect the voluntary interchange of data, information, experience, ideas, and knowledge about methods, processes, and techniques relating to investigations and security in advanced technologies among its membership. Visit the HTCIA website at https://htcia.org/.

Institute of Internal Auditors – The New York Chapter founded the Institute of Internal Auditors. Since then, the IIA has grown to serve members in internal auditing, governance, internal control, IT audit, education, and security from more than 160 countries/territories. The world's leader in certification, education, research, and technological guidance for the profession,.The Institute serves as the profession's watchdog and resource on significant auditing issues around the globe. Visit the website at https://na.theiia.org/Pages/IIAHome.aspx.

Intellectual Property Owners Association (IPO) – The IPO is a trade association for patents, trademarks, copyrights, and trade secrets. IPO is the only association in the U.S. that serves all intellectual property owners in all industries and all fields of technology. Visit the IPO website at http://www.ipo.org/.

International Anti-counterfeiting Coalition – The International Anti-counterfeiting Coalition is the world's largest non-profit organization devoted solely to protecting intellectual property and deterring counterfeiting. Our membership spans automotive, apparel, luxury goods, pharmaceuticals, and food, software, and entertainment. From small privately-owned companies to large multinationals, we share one common goal–to combat counterfeiting and piracy.

Visit the website at https://www.iacc.org/.

International Association for the Study of Organized Crime (IASOC) – The IASOC is a professional association of criminologists, researchers, working professionals, teachers, and students. IASOC promotes greater understanding and research about organized crime in all its manifestations. Visit the IASOC Twitter profile at https://twitter.com/theiasoc?lang=en.

International Association of Campus Law Enforcement Administrators (IACLEA) – The IACLEA advances public safety for educational institutions by providing educational resources, advocacy, and professional development services. IACLEA is the leading voice for the campus public safety community.

Visit the IACLEA website at http://www.iaclea.org/.

International Narcotic Enforcement Officers Association – INEOA (International Narcotic Enforcement Officers Association) is a non-profit membership organization representing the worldwide drug enforcement community. INEOA's principal purpose is to promote and foster cooperation, discussion, and interest in the global problems of narcotics trafficking and drug abuse. Visit the website at http://www.ineoa.org/.

National Association of Bail Enforcement Agents – This association aims to promote the principles and policies set forth within the bylaws to upgrade the profession and the professional. Visit the website at http://www.nabea.org/.

National Association of Certified Valuation Analysts – Supports the users of business and intangible asset valuation services and financial forensic services, including damages determinations of all kinds and fraud detection and prevention, by training and certifying financial professionals in these disciplines. NACVA training includes Continuing Professional Education (CPE) credit and is available to members and non-members. Visit the website at http://www.nacva.com/.

National Association of Drug Diversion Investigators (NADDI) – A non-profit organization that facilitates cooperation between law enforcement, healthcare professionals, state regulatory agencies, and pharmaceutical manufacturers in preventing and investigating prescription drug diversion. NADDI also sponsors and conducts specialized educational seminars and conferences. Visit the website at https://www.naddi.org/.

National Association of Fraud Investigators – Established to improve communications and to expand the networking of those in investigation and related fields, which include but is not limited to Law Enforcement, insurance investigators, professional investigators, security specialists, bond enforcement agents, attorneys, forensic examiners, tracers/locators, credit card investigators, auto theft investigators, international counterparts. Visit the website at http://www.nafraud.com/.

National Association of Legal Investigators – NALI was formed in 1967 for legal investigators actively engaged in negligence investigations for the plaintiff and/or criminal defense. Law firms, public defenders, or private investigative agencies may employ these investigators. Our primary focus is to educate and advance the art and science of legal investigation, and to ensure the highest standard of professional ethics. Visit the website at http://www.nali.com/.

National Association of Professional Accident Reconstruction Specialists – A non-profit organization whose members have joined together to share the challenge of dealing with the complex problems of accident reconstruction and to upgrade and ultimately professionalize the accident reconstruction field. Visit the website at

National Association of Professional Background Screeners – Founded in 2003 as a non-profit trade association, NAPBS® serves to represent the interest of companies offering tenant, employment, and background screening. NAPBS® offers an opportunity for qualified companies to participate in shaping the body of knowledge and regulations impacting our futures. Visit the website at https://thepbsa.org/.

National Association of Professional Process Servers (NAPPS) – A worldwide organization founded on the principles of professionalism and high ethical standards. Visit the website at http://www.napps.org/.

National White Collar Crime Center – Provides training, investigative support, and research to agencies and entities involved in the prevention, investigation, and prosecution of economic and high-tech crime. A non-profit membership organization dedicated to supporting Law Enforcement in preventing, investigating, and prosecuting economic and high-tech crime, NW3C has been continuously funded through competitive grants for over three decades. NW3C membership consists of Law Enforcement agencies from all 50 states and four continents. Visit the website at https://www.nw3c.org/.

Pacific Northwest Association of Investigators – A professional organization of licensed investigators incorporated in the State of Washington in December 1947. PNAI was established to encourage and assist members in their continuing professional education, and to establish goals for their professional conduct and behavior, by mandating standards of personal and professional conduct. Visit the website at http://www.pnai.com/.

Chapter 9: Conclusion

Working in the private investigation industry offers the opportunity for an exciting and rewarding career. Whether the case involves tracking down a lost loved one, uncovering the truth about a cheating spouse, or conducting a background check, private investigators provide essential services to individuals and businesses.

In addition, private investigation work provides a career path for individuals who previously worked in the military or law enforcement. The investigation industry is often the next logical step for those who wish to step out on their own.

Exploring a career in the industry may lead to other opportunities. For example, you may have a knack for tracking down subjects and decide to specialize as a skip tracer. Or, you may enjoy compiling background information and work history and thus you may decide to start a background investigation service. Whatever your motivation is for choosing this career field, you now have the basic framework for getting started. Start doing your research today to understand the training, education, and licensing requirements for your state.

I wish you the best in your new career.

Questions and Feedback

If you have any questions or feedback regarding this book's material, please email me at licensing@einvestigator.com.

If you have specific questions about private investigator licensing requirements or application processes, I highly recommend that you contact the licensing authority for the state in which you wish to be licensed.

Alternatively, you may wish to visit my website at www.einvestigator.com and post a comment on the appropriate state licensing page.

Reporting Errors, Discrepancies, and Omissions

This eBook is compiled from hundreds of sources, covering guidelines that are constantly changing. As such, some elements of the guide will be out of date the moment it is printed. The guide will be updated periodically to ensure it provides accurate and up--to-date information on licensing.

If you encounter any discrepancies between the information in this book and the state licensing website, the state website should be considered the most accurate information. The individual licensing authorities in each state govern the laws and regulations that pertain to private investigators.

I welcome your feedback and suggestions on how I can improve the guide. And if you notice any errors or omissions, please send me at licensing@einvestigator.com

###

About the Author

MICHAEL KISSIAH is the owner of Brandy Lane Publishing, LLC, which owns and operates a small portfolio of websites, including https://www.einvestigator.com. Michael created eInvestigator.com more than 20 years ago after working as a private investigator in the state of Florida. Since that time, he has become an expert at how to find information online and has written over 1000 articles on topics related to the investigation industry.

Follow eInvestigator.com on Twitter at http://twitter.com/einvestigation.

Follow eInvestigator.com on LinkedIn at https://www.linkedin.com/company/einvestigator-com/.

Friend eInvestigator.com on Facebook at http://facebook.com/einvestigator.

Disclaimers

Limit of Liability and Disclaimer of Warranty

Trademarks

Made in the USA
Las Vegas, NV
09 May 2024

89736395R00105